MW01514345

You and Your Whole House

Prayer and the salvation of your family

Fred Lambert

Copyright © 2022 Fred Lambert

All rights reserved.

ISBN: 978-1-7326263-1-7

DEDICATION

I dedicate this book to my beautiful wife Judy. In the following pages, I have chronicled a little bit of our love story and some of the truths and principles that we have learned together over the years. Thank you for believing in me, encouraging me, never giving up on me and for proofreading this book. ☺

I love you!

CONTENTS

ACKNOWLEDGMENTS

Thanks to Theresa Sutton – for praying for me when I was lost.

Thanks to Bob and Peggy Zide – I have learned so much from you.

Thanks to Fran Smith – my best man and a very cool follower of Jesus!

Thanks to Erwin and Petra Hehenberger – your story is the heart of this book and an inspiration to all.

Thanks to David and Sharon Ingles – you have strengthened Judy and me with your love, words of encouragement, prayers and support!

INTRODUCTION

"Can you pray for my husband? He doesn't know Jesus and gets upset when I go to church."

"Can you pray for my son? He grew up in church but lately he's been hanging around the wrong people. He refuses to come to church with me and I think he is taking drugs. Last week he told me that he doesn't believe in God anymore."

"Can you pray for my grandfather? He has liver cancer and the doctors said that there's nothing more they can do. They told us that he'll probably die in the next few weeks, but he doesn't know Jesus yet. He was an alcoholic most of his life and is such a hard man. He said that he can't believe that there's a God after the things he saw in the war. I don't want him to die without Jesus, but I don't know what to do."

These and many others like it are prayer requests of real people. Some of these prayer requests came from people who were recently saved and now they want to see their family members come to know Jesus. Others are from people who have lived for Jesus many years but haven't found the key to getting their family into the Kingdom of God.

There is good news for all of them and for all of us!

There is hope!

There is a promise!

There is a God Who wants your family saved!

Read the following two scriptures out loud and let them sink into your heart. Remember, faith comes by hearing the word of God.

Acts 16:31 So they said, "Believe on the Lord Jesus Christ, and you will be saved, you and your household."

Psalm 65:2 You who answer prayer, all people will come to You.

God is a God of families and a God who answers prayer! That's what this little book is about. There is a way to pray that releases the power of God's promises. There is power in every promise that God has made. Praying in faith activates that power!

When Judy and I got saved we told everyone in our family, all our friends and everyone we met about our new life! Most of them thought we had lost our minds. They couldn't relate. Many of them had preconceived ideas about God, Jesus and the church. A few of them who claimed to believe in life after death were of the opinion that somehow, they would be all right on their own. They reasoned, "I'm not a bad person. I never killed anyone. I never robbed a bank. I'm not as bad as others." What they didn't realize is that human standards of righteousness are like filthy rags in the eyes of God. (Isaiah 64:6) They don't realize that everyone needs Jesus! Everyone needs the Savior. They were blinded by the enemy of their soul just as Judy and I were before Jesus came into our lives.

But there is hope!

There is a promise!

There is a God with outstretched arms!

His arms are long enough to reach anyone - regardless of how far they may have strayed. He is reaching out to them right now!

Our God is a God of families and a God who answers prayer! He has given us clear directions in His word about how we can pray effectively for our families. Prayer is powerful! Prayer can open hearts, draw people to God, commission angels, schedule divine appointments and release revelation into the lives of those for whom we are praying. In other words, we can accomplish things when we pray that would be impossible to accomplish by our own efforts.

Since Judy and I got saved, many of our family members have received Jesus and the rest of them are on the way. We weren't always the people that God used to lead them to the Lord, but their salvation is an answer to our prayers and the prayers of others who interceded for them. Our dear friend David Ingles said, "You can pray your family into God's family."

Yes, you can!

Say this out loud, "I can pray my family into God's family."

You probably noticed that I said, "Many of our family members have received Jesus and the rest are on the way." I can say that with confidence because of God's promise and His great faithfulness. I believe that God will do everything necessary to bring them all into the Kingdom. I am acting on that belief, praying according to that belief and speaking in agreement with that belief. Because I believe in Jesus, I believe that my whole family will be saved.

You can believe that too!

Of course, some people are more stubborn than others and they resist God's love for various reasons. For example, my dad is not yet saved. But Judy and I already informed him that he can't die until he receives Jesus. The promise that "you and your house or family will be saved" belongs to us and to everyone who believes in Jesus! And we believe!

That doesn't mean that they are automatically saved. They're not. Nor does it mean that they don't have to make a personal decision for Jesus. They do. They'll have to open their hearts and receive Jesus just like everyone else. The promise does however mean, that we can trust God for their salvation! Our God is a God of families and a God who answers prayer!

It's my desire and hope that this book will encourage and equip you to pray more effectively for your family members as well as for those in your circle of influence who have yet to give their lives to Jesus. Your prayers are going to make a difference in their lives. To be saved, they must hear the gospel, believe it and receive Jesus but God uses our prayers to open their hearts and pave the way for their salvation. Never forget:

There is hope!

There is a promise!

There is a God who answers prayer!

And He loves your whole family!

Amen!

MY STORY: PART ONE

From Beethoven to the man in the red socks

"We've been praying five years for you, Freddy." That was the first thing I heard, when I went to church the first time after being saved. My sister's father-in-law was the one who said it. He was a very interesting man who loved Jesus with all his heart. He was a piano technician, a musician, a gospel singer, a kind and generous gentleman who wore red socks. When I asked him why he wore red socks, he said, "Because they remind me of the blood of Jesus!" I always thought that was both cool and funny at the same time! Thank God for the precious blood of Jesus and for their prayers. I was saved! When he said that they had been praying five years for me, I just smiled and said, "Well, it looks like it worked!"

Prayer works. Prayer changes things. Prayer unlocks doors and opens hearts. Prayer commissions angels and releases the power of God into people's lives. Prayer is an invitation from God to make use of His resources and change our world! People prayed for my salvation and here I am – saved and serving God! To fully appreciate that, you need to understand that I was the black sheep of my family. In my family, I was the least likely candidate to get saved.

For a school assignment when I was 12 years old, I read a biography about Ludwig Van Beethoven. I was young, highly impressionable, and that book radically influenced my life. From that time on, I wanted to be a classical musician and composer like my hero Beethoven.

My parents couldn't afford to send me to a music school or pay for piano lessons, so I started teaching myself. I worked in my uncle's hay fields and earned enough money to buy some piano method books. We didn't have a piano at home, but my mother had a small electric organ with a four-octave keyboard. It wasn't much but would play that thing for hours at a time. I barreled through books one and two and soon made it to book three. In book three, I learned how to play "Für Elise" by Beethoven. *(The easy part that everyone can play!)* ☺ I was so excited! I had arrived! I was a classical pianist. ☺ *(On that small electric organ.)*

I also began composing my own music. My first piece was a requiem. I didn't even know what a requiem was! I just knew that Mozart, Brahms and other classical composers had written requiems, so I thought that I should write one too. Without a doubt, it was the shortest and saddest requiem ever written but I was on the way to reaching my dreams.

In the middle of book three I got stuck. The lessons included some advanced syncopation. This was over my head – it was just too difficult for me to grasp as a 12-year-old self-learner. Lucky for me however, at the same time I reached that point where I couldn't go any further, my older sister brought home some albums from the Rolling Stones, Bob Dylan, Simon and Garfunkel, Cat Stevens and others. In addition to that, my older brother borrowed a guitar from someone and brought it home. I immediately recognized that rock-n-roll was a lot easier to play than classical music. My dream and goal in life changed overnight. From now on, I would be a rock-n-roller!

I played that guitar for hours on end. No one had to tell me to practice. Actually, my father thought that there was something wrong with me! He said, "Why aren't you outside playing baseball like a normal kid!" I was addicted to music! It was my passion. I started playing in bands when I was 13. We weren't very good, but we did our best to play like our heroes. "Stairway to Heaven", "Jumpin' Jack Flash", "I Wanna Hold Your Hand" were a few of the tunes we played.

We didn't just want to play like our heroes – we wanted to be like our heroes. I was 13 years old and I painted my fingernails black like Mick Jagger. I only did it once because my dad threatened my life for doing so and he was still bigger than me! He said, "No son of mine is going to be in a long haired, creepy rock band!" Of course, that just increased my determination, inspired my rebellious nature and made me want even more to be like the bad boys of rock and roll.

I secretly started smoking weed when I was 14 and drinking alcohol when I was 15. I couldn't do it all the time because I didn't have access to these things all the time. On weekends, me and my band mates would grab what we could find and get high or drunk or both. We were all growing musically and eventually our bands were good enough to get some gigs. We played at dances and parties and were living the dream. ☺

Although, I did well in school and generally got good grades, I never applied myself. Well-meaning people would say, "You need to study and learn so that you can get a good job." I told them I was going to be a rock star and didn't need all of that. They said, "But you might need something to fall back on in case it doesn't work out." I always countered, "I don't need anything to fall back on because I'm not planning to fall."

After I graduated from high school, I studied theater at a local university. At the same time, I was playing in a progressive rock band. The guys in the band wanted to go on the road and play full time. So, I dropped out of college and went on the road with them. I was 19 years old and the other guys were between the ages of 25-28. They were awesome musicians and I felt totally honored to be playing with them.

I learned the music and learned the routine. We'd play from 9 pm until 2 am and then party till the sun came up. Every night we'd sit around the table and pass joints around and drink like the world was coming to an end. This became my life and my lifestyle for the next 5 years.

During this time, I was in three different full time working bands. We played 6 nights a week 50 weeks per year. We had to beg to get time off. We played up and down the east coast and throughout the Midwest in casinos, resort hotels and freestanding show rooms. We opened for various big-name acts and had high hopes. Cocaine, Crystal Meth, Quaaludes, Valium, Black Beauties, Christmas Trees, LSD, and Magic Mushrooms were added to the menu. I eventually worked my way up to smoking 8 – 10 joints every day. I earned a lot of money, but spent about half of it on drugs, booze and cigarettes.

I was living the life.

I was imitating my heroes.

I was on my way to the big time!

Sex, drugs and rock-n-roll!

One of our gigs was in Ripley, Ohio. We played at a show room called the Riviera. It was the only club within 50 miles with live music. One evening during our first set, a very pretty girl named Judy came in. She had just turned 18. She came to the club with an older woman who was in a difficult marriage. When she sat down at a table in the front, I thought to myself, "I'm going to have to move fast on our break." There were 9 other guys in the band plus our roadie! When we finished the last song in our first set, I pretty much ran to her table and introduced myself. To make a long story short, we fell in love and a few weeks later, we moved in together. Some people called it living in sin, but I didn't care. I thought that sin was a part of my job description as a musician.

After a few years, my "rock-n-roll dream" turned into a job like any other job. We played in the casinos in Atlantic City, NJ about 6 months of year and the rest of the time we were on the road.

6 nights a week, 50 weeks a year. ☹

Every night it was pretty much the same thing. No one really came to hear our music. They came to drink, find a girl, find a guy or party – but they weren't there for us. As this reality dawned on me, the drugs and alcohol became more and more important. Many nights I overdid it to the point that I blacked out. Often on the mornings after, I couldn't remember anything that I had done the night before. Others died doing less but somehow, I survived.

I felt betrayed by life. My passion had become a boring job. My life had turned into a blurred, repetition of playing music without meaning – to people who didn't care – so that I could continue to get wasted afterward – and forget it all or at least ignore reality. One night we played at a club in South Jersey where they had a special called "TNT Night". Tacos and Tequila – three tacos for a dollar and two shots of tequila for a dollar. The tacos didn't interest me, but the tequila certainly did. We played and I took advantage of their special deal all night long. I stopped counting after 22 shots, which I had been washing down with beer. Our last show that night was not my best performance, to say the least.

After the gig, I got into an argument with the guys in the band and accused them of selling out. I was not in my right mind – I was mad, drunk as a skunk, and frustrated with my life. I smoked a joint and jumped in my big Cadillac Fleetwood to drive home. Everyone tried to convince me that I shouldn't drive. I could hardly stand up, let alone drive a car. Nonetheless, I cussed them out and got in my car and took off. It was a foggy night, and I had the pedal to the metal when I remembered that a sharp curve was coming up. My reaction time was extremely impaired, but I managed to slam on the brakes. The car slid on the wet asphalt, and I wound up in a ditch. My big car was messed up but there wasn't a scratch on my body! That was one of the many times where I could have easily been killed. Borderline overdoses, pushing the limits, driving drunk and high all the time was how I was living. I don't want to make it sound more dramatic than it was but like I said, others have died doing less.

And all this time,

people at First Assembly of God

in Millville, New Jersey

were praying for me.

I didn't know they were praying for me and wouldn't have cared if I had known it. I was an atheist. I thought Christians were dimwitted. To me, church was for little old ladies who were afraid of dying or for people who weren't that intelligent. I mocked Christians, gave them a hard time and intentionally tried to get them mad. I wanted to prove that they were just as messed up as me! I could be dead drunk at a party and if someone even mentioned the name of Jesus, I was ready to argue. I was a godless, immoral, nasty human being. I didn't love anyone except myself and at times I really hated him. I guess I loved Judy in a way but even that was a selfish love.

During Christmastime of 1983, Judy and I were at home drinking wine and singing Christmas carols. Because everybody sings Christmas carols at Christmas – even drug addict atheists! What happened that night changed my life forever. A friend had come to visit us, and we were partying and singing as loud as we could! I was accompanying us on guitar and playing out of an old Christmas songbook that had belonged to my grandfather. We were so loud and rowdy that the landlord knocked on the door and told us to quiet down. So we sang even louder!

Eventually, we came to a song that I had sung at least 100

times before. It was an old English Christmas carol called "God Rest Ye Merry Gentlemen". The arrangement had a lot of chords, so I had to pay extra attention to the music. We sang through the first verse and chorus and then something totally unexpected happened. It was life changing. It was overwhelming. I can't describe it in any other terms than this:

God touched my heart.

He made Himself real to me.

It took my breath away.

I sat there stunned.

I couldn't breathe.

Judy asked me if I was ok, but I couldn't respond. In that instant – in that very moment – I somehow realized that there is something special about Jesus. I didn't know what it was, but I knew that there was something I hadn't seen, heard or known before.

DON'T FORGET: People, who loved me, had been praying for me. My sister, her husband and the church that they attended were praying for me.

I started reading a small Bible that Judy had brought with her from Kentucky. I wouldn't recommend anyone else to read the Bible like I did. I'd smoke a joint and then read the Bible. I remember being so impressed with Jesus! "Wow dude! Check it out! Jesus is walking on the water! I don't know anybody else who can do that!" I'd take another hit, read a bit more and be totally blown away! "Whoa man! He's healing the sick! He's raising the dead! He's working miracles! Jesus is so cool!" It seemed like He loved to spend time with sinners – people like me! I'd take another drag and then read about how He gave the religious people a hard time! He called them hypocrites! I remember smoking that joint and saying, "Yeah Jesus! That's right! Those religious people are all hypocrites!"

And His words – those powerful words - no one else ever spoke like Jesus. His words resounded in my heart and rang of truth. No one else spoke words that cut through the façade of existence and revealed what life was all about as Jesus did.

During the next months, I read the Bible more than most Christians do. I also did more drugs than ever before. It was like there was a war being fought for my heart. On the one hand, I was getting to know Jesus. He had become my hero. On the other hand, the addictions and my filthy lifestyle were holding me back from committing to Him. About seven months later, on July 14,1984, all of that changed.

We had just finished playing our last show of the evening at Harrah's Casino. I planned to stay that night and play blackjack. Judy was visiting her folks in Kentucky, and I had a room at the casino. When I was combing my long brown hair and putting eye drops in my red eyes, it was as if the Lord said to me, "Fred, now you know the truth and look at how you're still living. I have something better for you than this." I was overwhelmed – again.

How could Jesus love me? I had mocked Him, cursed Him, mocked His people and fought against them. I was an immoral, godless, cigarette smoking, alcohol abusing, drug addict. Every second word from my mouth was a cuss word! How could He love me? I was touched by a love that I had never experienced anywhere else.

Our bass player was the only other person still in the room. He was raised Catholic and had recently rededicated his life to Jesus. He quit drinking, doing drugs and the other self-destructive things he had been doing. Although I was reading the Bible and thought Jesus was cool, I couldn't relate to all of that. I just thought he was going through some kind of a religious phase. But truth be told, he was happy and I wasn't. More than once, I mocked and argued with him and gave him a hard time. But there he was in room 424 at Harrah's Casino hotel the night that I gave my life to Jesus.

I asked him, "Franny, is it true that all you have to do to get saved, is to believe that God raised Jesus from the dead and confess Him as your Lord?" I had read this in the Bible and wanted to make sure that I understood it. Franny looked at me a little cautious because he wasn't sure if I was being sincere or just wanted to give him a hard time again. He said, "Yeah, that's all you have to do." Then I said, "Then I can be saved because I believe that Jesus is alive. I believe He is the Lord! He is the only one that I want to follow."

When I said this, I was born again.

Everything was somehow different.

It seemed like the very atmosphere had changed.

I can't remember if Franny prayed with me or not. The next day he told me that I cried like a baby! All I know is that the Holy Spirit came inside of me and made me a new person. It felt like a ton of bricks fell off my shoulders. Until this time, I didn't even know there was a ton of bricks on my shoulders! Like I said, it seemed like the very atmosphere was different. I was still in the casino, and everything still looked the same but somehow everything had changed.

I was saved.

I was born again.

I was a new creation!

I was a child of God.

Remember – don't forget – think about it – people had been praying for me. Family had been praying for me. God heard their prayers. He led me by His love to the point of decision and gave me grace to say yes to Jesus.

I'm telling you my story because I want to encourage you. No one is so far away from God that His long arms can't reach them. I was the least likely candidate in my family to get saved. I know that my family worried about me – especially my mom and sisters. But people kept praying for me and God finally got to me! Never forget, no matter what it looks like in the natural – no matter how far away our family members might be from God – He can still reach them! Our God is a God of families and a God who answers prayer.

No one on earth is beyond God's reach.

Not even the black sheep of your family!

You can pray your family into the family of God!

THE PROMISE

ACTS 16:30-31 *And he brought them out and said, "Sirs, what must I do to be saved?" So they said, "Believe on the Lord Jesus Christ, and you will be saved, you and your household."*

What a wonderful promise! If you believe in Jesus, God wants to save your whole family! He loves you and He loves everyone that you love! He knows what's important to you and wants to fulfill the deepest desires of your heart!

The background story to this promise is important.

Paul and Silas were thrown into prison for preaching the gospel and casting out demons. In the midnight hour, they were praying and praising God and it was loud enough for everyone else to hear. Suddenly an earthquake shook the prison. Everyone's chains fell to the ground and the prison doors swung wide open! The jailer was terrified! He knew that if the prisoners escaped, the governors would hold him responsible. Under Roman rule that would mean the death sentence for him. He pulled out his sword and was going to kill himself.

Paul sensed the urgency of the moment and called out, "Do yourself no harm, for we are all here." (Acts 16:28) The jailer came, threw himself down before Paul and Silas and asked,

"What must I do to be saved." Paul and Silas answered his question but they also answered a question that he didn't ask!

"Believe on the Lord Jesus and you will be saved – you and your whole house!"

He didn't ask, "How can my family and I be saved?" He wasn't thinking about his family at that moment! He was only thinking about his own life! But God was thinking about his family. Listen carefully: God is interested in us, but He is also interested in our whole family!

ACTS 16:32-34 *Then they spoke the word of the Lord to him and to all who were in his house. And he took them the same hour of the night and washed their stripes. And immediately he and all his family were baptized. Now when he had brought them into his house, he set food before them; and he rejoiced, having believed in God with all his household.*

Within a few hours, Paul had preached the gospel to the jailer and his whole family. They all were saved, just like God promised! That same night, they were all baptized. What joy! The jailer rejoiced with his whole family!

Jesus makes life worth living.

Jesus is the source of genuine joy!

Getting saved will make you happy.

Your whole family getting saved

will make you even happier! ☺

He went from fear, despair and the brink of suicide to great joy and rejoicing within a few short hours. What made the difference? Jesus Christ! He came into their lives, and they were changed. They were saved! They were set free from guilt and shame and their sins were forever washed away! Thank God for household salvation!

This Promise is to You and Your Family!

On the day of Pentecost, the Holy Spirit fell upon and filled those who were assembled in the upper room! God is on the lookout today for people with hungry hearts! Hungry hearts will be filled again and again. After they received the Spirit, a huge crowd of people came together. Peter took advantage of the situation! He preached the very first Gospel message of the church age. There's much to learn from that sermon but I want us to focus on how the people reacted and then see how Peter ministered to them.

ACTS 2:37-39 *Now when they heard this, they were cut to the heart, and said to Peter and the rest of the apostles, "Men and brethren, what shall we do?" Then Peter said to them, "Repent, and let every one of you be baptized in the name of Jesus Christ for the remission of sins; and you shall receive the gift of the Holy Spirit. For the promise is to you and to your children, and to all who are afar off, as many as the Lord our God will call."*

The power of the Holy Spirit was heavy and people were deeply convicted. They were "cut to the heart". They knew that they needed help! This is what we need today to reach the confused masses who have been lied to and deceived all their lives. We need more of the convicting power of the Holy Spirit!

They cried out, "Men and brethren, what shall we do?" Peter didn't hesitate. He knew what they needed to do. He said, *"Repent, and let every one of you be baptized in the name of Jesus Christ for the remission of sins; and you shall receive the gift of the Holy Spirit."* Amen! Jesus is the way, the truth and the life. He is the only source of salvation.

Now notice that just like the Philippian jailer, these folks didn't ask about how their families could be saved. They asked, *"What must we do?"* And like Paul and Silas, Peter answered their question as well as the question they didn't ask.

"For the promise is to you and to your children, and to all who are afar off, as many as the Lord our God will call."

They were overcome with conviction and their only thought was about how they could be saved. However, when they asked for instructions, God was already thinking about their whole family.

He loves your children, your grandchildren, your mom, your dad, your brothers, your sisters, your wife, your husband, your aunts, your uncles, your cousins, your nephews, your nieces and everyone in your whole family! Believe on the Lord Jesus Christ and your will be saved and your whole house!

The Father Heart of God

Jesus revealed God as a loving Heavenly Father who longs to meet the needs of mankind. His love is so deep and passionate for humanity that He sent His own Son to die in our place. He is the Father of spirits and the Father of the family of God. He created humanity out of His heart's desire for a family.

In one sense, God has no needs at all. He is perfect and complete just the way He is. But He wanted someone that He could pour out His love upon. He desired someone to fellowship with, someone to spend time with and someone with whom He could share His greatness. The heart of God is the heart of a loving Father. The purposes of God are manifold but His primary reason for creating man was His heart's desire for a family.

We need to know this well. Many people have a false image of God which is based upon:

Dead religious traditions,

    poor parental role models

        or the continual condemnation of the devil.

Some think of God as no more than an uncaring bully. They see Him as a judge Who is waiting for the first opportunity to punish them. They imagine that God has a great big baseball bat and that He's waiting for the first opportunity to beat them over the head with it. They think that God is looking forward to the day when He can throw all the sinners into hell.

I used to think like that until I started reading the Bible and listening to what Jesus said about God. Jesus spoke of God as a loving Father who knows our needs. He is concerned about us. He wants to provide for us. He wants to help us.

MATTHEW 6:7-8 *And when you pray, do not use vain repetitions as the heathen do. For they think that they will be heard for their many words. "Therefore do not be like them. For your Father knows the things you have need of before you ask Him.*

You don't have to talk God into doing something for you. You don't have to persuade Him to give you the things you need. He is a Father who generously gives good gifts to His children.

MATTHEW 7:11 *If you then, being evil, know how to give good gifts to your children, how much more will your Father who is in heaven give good things to those who ask Him!*

He's a good God

and He gives good gifts!

Paul referred to God as the Father of the whole family in Heaven and earth.

EPHESIANS 3:14-15 *For this reason I bow my knees to the Father of our Lord Jesus Christ, of whom the whole family in heaven and earth is named.*

He said that the Father Himself qualified us to be partakers of the inheritance of the saints in light!

COLOSSIANS 1:12 *giving thanks to the Father who has qualified us to be partakers of the inheritance of the saints in the light.*

19

The Father is not condemning us. He's not holding things back from us. He has qualified us and generously given us a glorious inheritance in Christ!

James, the brother of Jesus, said that God the Father gives exclusively good and perfect gifts to His children. He said it in simple terms so that we won't be deceived.

JAMES 1:16-18 *Do not be deceived, my beloved brethren. Every good gift and every perfect gift is from above, and comes down from the Father of lights, with whom there is no variation or shadow of turning. Of His own will He brought us forth by the word of truth, that we might be a kind of firstfruits of His creatures.*

Many people are deceived and think that God is an angry judge. They feel like they could never be good enough for Him. They rebel against Him and run from Him because they feel condemned and unwanted. But this is a false picture - an incorrect understanding of who our Father in heaven truly is. He sent His Son to pay the penalty that we all deserved because of His great love for all humanity. James tells us that He did this of His own will. He chose to do it. He wanted to restore us so desperately that He paid the debt and penalty that we owed.

Jesus died a horrible, painful death. He was made sin with our sins. He was made sick with our sicknesses and pains. He became poor with our poverty because the heart of the Father longed to restore our broken relationship and make us healthy, whole and rich. Don't be deceived. God loves you more than you can imagine, and He loves your family just as passionately. He never changes and His love never ends.

He is our loving Heavenly Father, and He knows firsthand –and on a very large scale – what it is like to have a family. Entire books have been written about the Father heart of God, but the parable of the prodigal son reveals His heart more than any other words we could ever hear. What Jesus revealed about God the Father in this parable is shockingly good yet still unknown to so many people.

God the Father knows the pain of having a family member go astray. In the parable of the prodigal son, we see how God longs for the return of wayward family members.

LUKE 15:11-12 *Then Jesus said: "A certain man had two sons. And the younger of them said to his father, 'Father, give me the portion of goods that falls to me.' So, he divided to them his livelihood.*

The story begins with an incident that would have offended everyone listening. The son of a rich man asks his father to pay out the inheritance that he would normally get after his father's death. He wasn't especially polite or humble about it when he asked. He didn't even say, "Please". He just demanded "his part" of the inheritance as if the father owed it to him. "Give me what you owe me dad!"

For the people listening as Jesus spoke, this would be paramount to saying, "I can't want to wait for you to die, I want my money now." In other words, "I don't care about you, this family, this house or anything else. I just want to cash in my inheritance and get out of here." He didn't want a relationship; he only wanted the material benefits.

Try to imagine the pain and disgrace that the father experienced. Children in both the Old and New Covenants are commanded to obey and honor their parents. If a child was unruly and disrespectful to his parents, they could be stoned according to the law of the Old Covenant. What would the neighbors say about such a son? How would they talk about the father if he acquiesced to his son's disrespectful request? If he didn't punish the son for his blatant disrespect, it could bring shame on the whole family. Maybe other children in the village would follow suit. People would talk! For a Jewish father under the law, this was a great dishonor! But he simply swallowed the shame, gave his unthankful son his part of the inheritance and let him go.

LUKE 15:13-16 *And not many days after, the younger son gathered all together, journeyed to a far country, and there wasted his possessions with prodigal living. But when he had spent all, there arose a severe famine in that land, and he began to be in want. Then he went and joined himself to a citizen of that country, and he sent him into his fields to feed swine. And he would gladly have filled his stomach with the pods that the swine ate, and no one gave him anything.*

He demanded his inheritance, took the money and left home. Within a short time, he had wasted his inheritance on pleasure – eating, drinking, sleeping with various prostitutes, partying with his so-called friends. He had no respect for what the inheritance represented. His father had worked hard to provide for his family. He was conscientious and saved to provide for his children's future. All of this meant nothing to the son. He was only interested in having a good time and fulfilling his selfish desires.

Eventually the money ran out. A fool and his money will soon be parted! He began to experience hardship for the first time in his life. He had nothing to eat. He was reduced to feeding a herd of pigs for room and board. For a Jew, this was about as low as you could go. He was feeding those stinky, ceremonially unclean pigs and was so hungry that he wanted to eat their food. The more Jesus spoke, the more repulsive the son became in the minds of the hearers.

LUKE 15:17-19 *But when he came to himself, he said, 'How many of my father's hired servants have bread enough and to spare, and I perish with hunger! I will arise and go to my father, and will say to him, "Father, I have sinned against heaven and before you, and I am no longer worthy to be called your son. Make me like one of your hired servants."*

He came to his senses and remembered how good he had it in his father's home. Sometimes people must experience the fruit of their doings to get to this place. He "came to himself" and concocted what he thought would be a clever plan. His father's servants were treated better than he was being treated. They were eating better than he was eating. He decided to return home, pretend to humble himself before his father and ask to become one of his servants.

He knew that what he had done was wrong. He realized that he had disgraced and dishonored his father but that's not the reason that he was sorry. He felt sorry that his father's servants were better off than he was. His motives were not true repentance and humility but rather selfishness. He wasn't going home because he loved and missed his father. He was hungry and wanted to get out of the mess into which he had gotten himself. So, he rehearsed his speech and headed home.

Father, I have sinned against heaven and you.

I am no longer worthy to be called your son.

Let me be as one of your hired servants.

LUKE 15:20-21 *And he arose and came to his father. But when he was still a great way off, his father saw him and had compassion, and ran and fell on his neck and kissed him. And the son said to him, "Father, I have sinned against heaven and in your sight, and am no longer worthy to be called your son."*

The story doesn't indicate any rushing or hurrying on the part of the son. He was probably somewhat afraid to go home. How would he be received? Maybe he wasn't sure that his plan would work. He had disgraced his father. Maybe his father wouldn't forgive him. He certainly had doubts and fears. I can imagine that he was worrying about what might happen the whole way home.

Jesus said that the father saw him and recognized him "when he was a great way off". He hadn't forgotten any detail about his son. He knew what his son looked like. He remembered how tall he was. He knew how he walked. The story implies that the father had been waiting, looking and longing for the day when his son would return. He sat at the gate of the city watching and waiting in hope.

The son was only walking but as soon as his father saw him, he jumped up and ran to meet him. Normally, the children were supposed to run to their parents. If the parents called, the children were expected to come immediately and quickly. Important people in those days didn't run. If they had to do something in a hurry, they would send one of their servants to run and do it. But this father's love was so passionate that he jumped up and ran to meet his son.

He threw his arms around his son and kissed him. The son was most likely still dressed in the dirty, filthy rags he wore as a pig keeper. He most likely stunk just like a pig. None of that mattered to the father. When he saw his son, he didn't see a filthy, stinky pig feeder. He saw his precious boy. He looked at him with eyes of love and embraced him. He didn't even let his son finish the speech he had prepared. He interrupted him before he even got to ask his question.

LUKE 15:22-24 *But the father said to his servants, "Bring out the best robe and put it on him, and put a ring on his hand and sandals on his feet. And bring the fatted calf here and kill it, and let us eat and be merry; for this my son was dead and is alive again; he was lost and is found.' And they began to be merry.*

How did the father treat his son who left his family for a life of sin? What did he do to his son who had dishonored him and wasted his inheritance on wild living?

- He hugged him.
- He kissed him.
- He restored him to his position.
- He gave him clean, new clothes.
- He gave him his signet ring.
- He gave him new shoes for his tired and dirty feet.
- He was so happy that he threw a great party.
- He celebrated.

- He brought out the best food and drink.
- He hired a band.
- He made a speech about how much he loves his son.
- He rejoiced!

This is a picture of the heart of our Heavenly Father. He longs for the salvation of every lost sinner. The heart of the Father is always on the lookout for the return of His wayward children. His love for them is passionate and never ending. He is waiting, looking, longing and hoping for their return.

When they come home, He runs to meet them. He doesn't wait for them to come, bow down, tell Him how bad they've been and how sorry they are. He doesn't condemn them. He is not spiteful. He is not a mean-hearted judge. As soon as they turn to Him, He hugs them. He cleanses them and gives them robes of righteousness. He restores to them their place in the family. He gives them the ring of His authority to use in life. He gives them shoes to protect their tired and sore feet from the hard and rocky roads they must travel in this world.

And then He celebrates!

LUKE 15:10 *Likewise, I say to you, there is joy in the presence of the angels of God over one sinner who repents."*

What a wonderful, loving Father! His heart is full of love and compassion for those who have lost their way. It is not His will that any perish. He doesn't rejoice when people die and go to hell. He rejoices when people return home and get saved.

2 PETER 3:9 *The Lord is not slack concerning His promise, as some count slackness, but is longsuffering toward us, not willing that any should perish but that all should come to repentance.*

The Father heart of God is full of love, compassion, forgiveness and mercy.

PSALM 86:5 *For You, Lord, are good, and ready to forgive, and* *abundant in mercy to all those who call upon You.*

He wants all people to be saved and come to know the wonderful things that He has prepared for them. There is a place in His house for everyone who wants to come home.

JOHN 14:2 *In My Father's house are many mansions; if it were not so, I would have told you. I go to prepare a place for you*

No matter how bad they may have been, no matter how disrespectful and dishonoring they have been, He loves them with an unconditional, perfect and never-ending love.

ROMANS 5:8 *But God demonstrates His own love toward us, in that while we were still sinners, Christ died for us.*

Jesus told the parable of the prodigal son to reveal how much God the Father loves the lost and the wayward. He continues to love people even though they don't deserve it. He doesn't call for the village to stone them, He calls upon us all to recognize that true love is bigger than any sin or any disgrace!

Just a side thought here, this father was a good father. Maybe you're reading this book and you weren't always a good father or a good mother. Maybe your children have left and don't call or want any contact with you. I want you to know that there is hope in Christ. The promise, "You and your house will be saved" belongs to you too. You may have to call them, write them, humble yourself and ask for forgiveness but things can change if you pray for them and follow God's leadings.

God Wants all People to be Saved

Yes, God wants to save your whole family! He desires it! He said it repeatedly. He not only wants to save our family, and us but He desires that all people would be saved!

1 TIMOTHY 2:3-4 *For this is good and acceptable in the sight of God our Savior, who desires all men to be saved and to come to* *the knowledge of the truth.*

You can't say it any clearer than that! God wants all people to be saved! That includes your whole family!

ISAIAH 55:1 *Ho! Everyone who thirsts, come to the waters; and you who have no money, come, buy and eat. Yes, come, buy wine and milk without money and without price.*

His call goes out to all people – to everyone who is thirsty! Come and drink! Come and eat at the table that God Himself has prepared! There is room for everyone at His table!

As we read in **2 Peter 3:9**, God is not willing that any perish! This is not what He wants. He wants them to turn to Him and be saved. Our wonderful Father wants all His wayward children to come back home.

EZEKIEL 33:11 *Say to them: 'As I live,' says the Lord GOD,'I have no pleasure in the death of the wicked, but that the wicked turn from his way and live. Turn, turn from your evil ways! For why should you die, O house of Israel?'*

Listen to the Father pleading, *"Turn, turn, from your evil ways and come home!"* It never makes God happy when people die in their sins. It breaks His heart. He doesn't want them to perish and be separated from Him. He wants them to repent and turn from the ways that lead to death. He wants them to get on the road that leads to the eternal dwelling he has prepared for them.

ISAIAH 45:22 *Look to Me, and be saved, all you ends of the earth! For I am God, and there is no other.*

It doesn't matter where they are or what they are doing. His arm is not too short to save! He is looking for them and He calls them to look to Him and be saved.

JOHN 3:16-17 *For God so loved the world that He gave His only begotten Son, that whoever believes in Him should not perish but* *have everlasting life. For God did not send His Son into the world to condemn the world, but that the world through Him might be saved.*

God so loved the whole world. That means every person, every nation, every tribe, every people group. He didn't send Jesus to condemn the world but to save it. This is for every "whosoever"! You are a "whosoever". All your family members are "whosoevers"! Everyone you know or ever will know is a "whosoever!"

TITUS 2:11 *For the grace of God that brings salvation has appeared to all men.*

His grace has appeared to all people because He wants all people to be saved. Salvation is a gift of grace. *For by grace you have been saved through faith, and that not of yourselves; it is the gift of God,* **(EPHESIANS 2:8)** God's grace extends to all people. It is unlimited. His grace has appeared to all people because it is for all people. God wants all people to be saved. That's His desire. That's the heart of the Father.

These and many other scriptures make it clear that God wants all people to be saved. But God places special priority on the salvation of your family.

God *IS NOT* a Respecter of Persons

ACTS 10:34 *Then Peter opened his mouth, and said, "Of a truth I perceive that God is no respecter of persons"*

God sent Peter supernaturally to Caesarea to preach the good news to Cornelius and his family. An angel appeared to Cornelius and told him to send for Peter. The angel told him where to find Peter and even the name and occupation of the person with whom he was staying. We will talk more about angels later but for now let's just say that we can believe God for angelic help in the salvation of our families.

Peter had a supernatural experience that we read about in this story. While he was praying, he received a vision. In the vision he saw animals that according to the law, Jewish people were not allowed to eat. A voice told him to kill and eat the animals. His religious sensibilities were offended, and he said, *"No, Lord. Nothing unclean or common has ever entered my mouth"*. But God said to him, *"Don't call anything unclean that I have cleansed."*

In the Old Testament, salvation was only for the Jews. If a Gentile wanted to be saved, they had to convert to Judaism. With this vision, God was explaining to Peter that in the New Covenant, all people can come to God just as they are. They don't have to convert to Judaism. They don't have perform religious rituals or earn His favor by heaping up good works. They simply come to Jesus, receive Him and their faith activates the grace that saves them. I like to say it this way, "We come as we are, and He makes us into what we should be!"

With this fresh revelation, Peter preached the Gospel to Cornelius and his family, and they were all saved!

ROMANS 2:11 *For there is no respect of persons with God.*

Some people think that the promise in **Acts 16:31** – *"Believe on the Lord Jesus Christ and you'll be saved and your house"* – was only for the Philippian jailer. But ask yourself this: Did God love the Philippian jailer and his family more than He loves you and your family? Of course not! Would He make a promise to one of His children that He wouldn't make to another? No! Does God have favorite children? Again, the answer is no!

God is no respecter of persons. If it was God's will for the Philippian jailer and his household to be saved, then it is also His will for you and your household to be saved!

- God loves all people!
- He loves Jews and Gentiles.
- He loves Muslims, Hindus and Buddhists.

- He loves people of all races and skin colors.
- He loves people of all nationalities.
- He loves people of every ethnic group.
- He loves people from every family.
- He loves sinners and saints.

He loves us all with His perfect, unconditional and never-ending love! While we were yet sinners, Christ died for us. This proves that His love for us is unconditional.

When I was growing up, the Rolling Stones were one of my favorite bands. They were called the "bad boys of rock-n-roll". In an interview once, Keith Richards (guitarist and song writer) was asked, "What do you think about the phrase, 'Sex, Drugs and Rock-n-roll'". He said, "I don't think anything about it. I invented it."

He wrote an autobiography and titled it, "Life". Several years ago, I found it in an airport bookstore for half price. I bought it and read it. I'm not recommending that anyone else read it but I did. The book has a lot of language that we as Christians don't use – or at least we shouldn't use. There are also a lot of stories of what we would refer to as sinful behavior in the book. It's a big book. It has 564 pages. I think it took me a total of 24 hours over a period of two weeks to read it.

Like I said, there were a lot of things in the book that would shock most Christians but there were also some very humorous and interesting anecdotes. I got to know Keith Richards in a way that I hadn't known him before. A lot of what people think about him is really based more upon myths and the image that he projects as a rock-roll star. Don't get me wrong, he certainly earned the title of "bad boy of rock-n-roll", but he is also a loving husband and father. He is a fiercely loyal friend. He is a very gifted guitarist and songwriter who is truly committed to his art. He is a man who has thoughts about life, justice and even eternity. His wife is a born again Christian but he's still not so sure what he believes. One thing is for certain, he hopes that there is a place after this life, where he will see family and friends who have passed on before him.

At the end of the book, I realized that I really like this guy! Like a ton of bricks, it hit me:

God loves people like Keith Richards!

He loves them so much that He sent Jesus to make the way for them to be saved and have eternal life!

Sometimes we only see the outward shell or the projected image of a person. God sees their heart. He doesn't only see the bad things. He doesn't only see their sin. He sees their gifts, their good traits, their hopes and their dreams. After reading this book, it was easier for me to understand why God loves all people. They truly are loveable in so many ways. They are precious and valuable in a way that far exceeds the value of any other created thing.

As a side note, I remember thinking that those 24 hours were the most time that I had spent with a lost person in a long time. For most of us Christians, we develop our own little microcosm and only hang out with people of like precious faith. For me as a pastor this is even more so! While it is good and right to have fellowship with people who believe like we do and encourage and strengthen one another, it is also important that we intentionally reach out to those who do not yet have the hope that we have.

God loves all people.

God wants all people to be saved.

Even the bad boys of rock-n-roll.

Even people like Keith Richards.

God *IS* a Respecter of Persons

On the one hand, God is no respecter of persons. As

we've seen, He wants ALL people to be saved. On the other hand, your family has a special place in God's heart because of His relationship with you. Your family has a special place in the heart of God.

In First Corinthians chapter seven, Paul talks about sex and marriage. He was a happy and healthy single. He said that he wished everyone could be like him. He knew, however that each person has his or her own gift. Most people do not have the gift of celibacy. If you can't say like Paul, "I wish that everyone was like me" then you probably don't have this gift! ☺ If you feel lonely and are envious of everyone who is happily married or has a partner, this is definitely not your gift! ☺

Among other things, Paul talks about believers who are married to unbelievers. His take on the matter – inspired by the Holy Spirit – is that if a Christian is married to an unbeliever, the Christian shouldn't divorce the unbeliever simply because of their unbelief. If the unbeliever loves them and is happy in the marriage, then a good Christian should be the best husband or wife to them that they can be. Listen to the powerful, hope-filled statement that Paul makes amid this teaching:

1 CORINTHIANS 7:12-14 *But to the rest I, not the Lord, say: If any brother has a wife who does not believe, and she is willing to live with him, let him not divorce her. And a woman who has a husband who does not believe, if he is willing to live with her, let her not divorce him. For the unbelieving husband is sanctified by the wife, and the unbelieving wife is sanctified by the husband; otherwise your children would be unclean, but now they are holy.*

The unbelieving husband is sanctified by the faith of his believing wife. We could also say that an unbelieving wife is sanctified by the faith of her believing husband. They are sanctified.

What does that even mean? The Bible has a lot of words that people don't really understand. "Sanctified" is one of them.

"Sanctified" means "set apart for God". It means that something or someone is placed in a special category. In other words, the unbelieving husband is set apart for God or put into a special category with God because of his wife's faith. Your unbelieving family members have a special place in the heart of God. He can do special things for them because of your faith!

"Sanctified" does not mean that they are automatically saved but it does mean that they have a special relationship with God because of your faith. There are special things He can do for them. He will draw them, open their hearts, protect them, show Himself strong on their behalf because of you. God loves all people, but He will do special things for your yet to be saved family members because of your faith – because you are His child!

Take this with you.

Never forget it.

Your family is special to God.

God is Touched by What Touches You

As a believer, you have a special standing with God. You are no longer alone in this world. The things that you face you do not face alone. Your problems are no longer yours alone. They are also God's problems. Your needs and desires touch the very heart of God.

1 CORINTHIANS 6:17 *But he that is joined unto the Lord is one spirit.*

Through the new birth you have become one spirit with the Lord. You are joined together with the Father of spirits. Being in direct union with God means that He is ever aware of your needs and desires. When something touches your heart, it touches the Father's heart as well.

JOHN 14:20 *At that day you will know that I am in My Father, and you in Me, and I in you.*

Jesus is in the Father, we are in Him and He is in us. This means that the Father is in us as well. Everything we go through, everything we experience, everything we feel, He is right there going through it with us. Because of this, your family has a special place in His heart. And because of this He wants to do special things to get their attention and call them into His kingdom!

You are one with God or united with God through the New Covenant sealed in Jesus' very own blood. An understanding of the blood covenant is important to growing a strong faith life. Our Covenant with God also reveals why our family is so important to Him. So, let's look at our covenant with God.

COVENANT RIGHTS

To understand our relationship with God, we must understand the word "covenant". In the Bible, God made covenants with various people. A covenant is a sacred and binding agreement between two parties. The ancient peoples respected and honored covenants in a way that is hard for us to understand today. In our world, people sign contracts one day and break them the next day. For the ancients, to break a covenant was unthinkable.

They understood the power of words and the power of promises. If you had given someone your word and made promises to them, you were bound to keep them. You had become one with that person. Their life was your life, and your life was their life. To break a covenant would be paramount to lying to yourself or abandoning yourself.

In a covenant relationship, everything you own becomes the rightful property of your covenant partner and everything they own becomes yours. It is much more than a contract. In a blood covenant, the two parties literally become one.

This is why I believe that prenuptial agreements are always wrong. Marriage is a covenant and the two people become one! Today, people want to marry someone, but they want to maintain property in their own name. That's not what a marriage is. They marry with the thought in their head that there's a good chance they might get divorced. Planning for failure makes failing easy. That should not be our goal in marriage! Marriages like that are doomed from the start.

If you can't give your whole life – everything you are – everything you own – everything you will ever be – to the person you are marrying, then you shouldn't get married. And if you don't want to get married, you shouldn't be having sex! That's an entirely different subject but it also one of the biggest problems in our society today.

Sex is something to be enjoyed (yes, enjoyed!) exclusively in the marriage relationship between one man and one woman who are completely committed to each other by covenant vows. "Till death do us part" has a real justification. Anything less than this disappoints and devalues sexuality.

Sex is pleasurable and that's good, but it is more than mere pleasure. It is a covenant act and joins people together in the deepest way. Two people become one in ways that transcend the physical act of sex. One gives a precious and valuable part of their soul to the other person in the act of sexual intercourse. This explains why there are so many broken people walking around wondering what went wrong. They gave a precious part of themselves to another person and the relationship was shattered and broken. That part of themselves that they gave, they can never get back. Sometimes they move on from one person to the next, always leaving a part of themselves behind and wind up broken, shattered and empty themselves.

Sex is exclusively for those who are in a covenant relationship with one another through marriage. This is God's design. That which they give to each other is never lost. It is honored, cherished and greatly valued by the one they love – by the one with whom they are in covenant.

In the ancient times, covenants were generally sealed or ratified with blood. The blood of the one party was mixed with the blood of the other party. Sometimes this was done symbolically with the blood of animals. Blood is representative of life. Two lives were mixed together – they were joined together. The result was one new life!

Blessings were pronounced for all who kept the covenant as well as curses for those who would dare break it. A blood covenant was a sacred and binding union. It always included more than the persons involved in the actual covenant ritual. The covenant promises applied in full to every member of the tribe or every member of the family for all generations.

As we look at the Old Testament, we see that God instituted a variety of covenants. These covenants served as forerunners of the New Covenant, which He established in Jesus Christ. The covenants He sanctioned always included the families of His covenant partners. One of the men He chose to make covenant with was Abraham.

GENESIS 15:8 *On the same day the LORD made a covenant with Abram, saying: To your descendants I have given this land, from the river of Egypt to the great river, the River Euphrates:*

God made a covenant with Abram (who later became Abraham). Notice that the covenant included promises for his children that were yet to be born. *"To your descendants I have given this land."* The covenant also included and provided blessings for Abraham's wife.

GENESIS 17:15-16 *Then God said to Abraham, "As for Sarai your wife, you shall not call her name Sarai, but Sarah shall be her name. And I will bless her and also give you a son by her; then I will bless her, and she shall be a mother of nations; kings of peoples shall be from her."*

God's covenants always included the whole family!

He said, "I will bless you.

I will bless your wife.

I will bless your children!"

Over the years, I've had personal dealings with all kinds of families – and believe me – it's better to have a blessed husband, blessed wife and blessed kids than ones who are not! ☺ And that's exactly what you get when you understand the covenant you have with God.

Later, the covenant promises and blessings were passed on to Abraham's son Isaac. God spoke to Isaac:

GENESIS 26:3-4 *Dwell in this land, and I will be with you and bless you; for to you and your descendants I give all these lands, and I will perform the oath which I swore to Abraham your father. And I will make your descendants multiply as the stars of heaven; I will give to your descendants all these lands; and in your seed all the nations of the earth shall be blessed.*

Notice again, *"You and your descendants will be blessed!"* When God sees you, He sees every generation of your family! Many years later, God spoke to Isaac's son Jacob and renewed the covenant and pronounced the blessing.

GENESIS 28:13-14 *And behold, the LORD stood above it (the ladder) and said: "I am the LORD God of Abraham your father and the God of Isaac; the land on which you lie I will give to you and your descendants. Also your descendants shall be as the dust of the earth; you shall spread abroad to the west and the east, to the north and the south; and in you and in your seed all the families of the earth shall be blessed*

The covenant blessings are for our whole family. They are for our immediate family and for all our descendants from one generation to the next. Of course, our children and grandchildren must grow and develop in their own relationship with God.

No one is automatically saved just because their parents have a covenant with God. The covenant gives them a special place before God but every generation must open their hearts and receive Him. The old saying, "God has no grandchildren, He only has children" is true. But the covenant that God made with you has promises for your whole family!

We must raise our children to know the Lord. It's not an easy task in the world in which we live, but it is possible. No one is perfect except Jesus and there is no perfect parent except God the Father – but Jesus and the Father will help us when we fail or make mistakes. Don't give up! Remember that the salvation of your family is a covenant promise from God Himself.

PSALM 112:1-2 *Blessed is the man who fears the LORD, who delights greatly in His commandments. His descendants will be mighty on earth; the generation of the upright will be blessed.*

The covenant is powerful and contains promises, blessings and provisions for you, your family and the coming generations. At a prayer meeting many years ago, the Lord gave me a prophetic word and said, "Your children will run faster, build bigger and accomplish more than you." We have seen this come to pass in the lives of our children.

Say this over your children:

My children

will run faster,

build bigger,

and accomplish more than me.

We've seen that God's covenant with Abraham included powerful promises for Abraham's immediate family and his descendants to all generations. What about his other family members? What about family members outside of the immediate family?

What about Aunts, Uncles, Nieces and Nephews?

There's a lot that we can learn from the story of Abraham's nephew Lot. When God called Abraham to leave his "father's house", the implication was that he should have left Lot behind too. But he didn't. He took Lot with him and Lot caused a lot of problems for Abraham. Having a covenant with God doesn't ensure that you will never have some challenges in your family. However, it does mean that God will help you overcome the challenges!

God blessed Abraham just like He promised! He became a very wealthy man. He had great herds of livestock and plenty of gold and silver. God also blessed Lot – and for no other reason than the fact that he was Abraham's nephew. In this, we see that the blessing of the covenant reaches farther than our immediate family.

GENESIS 13:5-6 *Lot also, who went with Abram, had flocks and herds and tents. Now the land was not able to support them, that they might dwell together, for their possessions were so great that they could not dwell together.*

The herdsmen of Abraham and Lot began to argue and fight because the land was not big enough to support all of them and their herds. To put an end to the strife, Abraham decided that it would be best for them to go their separate ways. Abraham – always the generous giver – allowed Lot to choose the direction in which he wanted to go.

GENESIS 13:10-11 *And Lot lifted his eyes and saw all the plain of Jordan, that it was well watered everywhere (before the LORD destroyed Sodom and Gomorrah) like the garden of the LORD, like the land of Egypt as you go toward Zoar. Then Lot chose for himself all the plain of Jordan, and Lot journeyed east. And they separated from each other.*

Lot looked at everything and chose the best land for himself. At least that's what he thought. Never forget this: things that look good outwardly are not always good in reality. Not only that, but selfishness will always lead us in the wrong direction.

GENESIS 13:12-13 *Abram dwelt in the land of Canaan, and Lot dwelt in the cities of the plain and pitched his tent even as far as Sodom. But the men of Sodom were exceedingly wicked and sinful against the LORD.*

Abraham allowed Lot to choose and Lot selfishly chose what looked to be the best. Later, after Lot left, God told Abraham to look at all the land all around him, which of course would include the land that Lot chose.

GENESIS 13:14-17 *And the LORD said to Abram, after Lot had separated from him: "Lift your eyes now and look from the place where you are — northward, southward, eastward, and westward; for all the land which you see I give to you and your descendants forever. And I will make your descendants as the dust of the earth; so that if a man could number the dust of the earth, then your descendants also could be numbered. Arise, walk in the land through its length and its width, for I give it to you."*

Lot chose what he thought was the best and later lost it all. Abraham was willing to give the best and later God gave it all to him! Even though Lot was obviously selfish and even though he lived in a place that is eternally known for perversion and wickedness, God didn't give up on him. Lot was Abraham's nephew and Abraham had a covenant with God!

In Genesis 14, four kings joined together and went to war against the King of Sodom and four other kings that had made an alliance with him. Four kings against five kings and the four kings won the battle. They plundered Sodom and Gomorrah and while they were at it, they took Lot, his family and all his possessions too.

When Abraham heard about it, he took 318 of his trained

41

servants and went to rescue Lot. Abraham was primarily a herdsman or a farmer. But this farmer went with his servants – *and with the God of the covenant* – and defeated four kings and their armies and rescued his nephew Lot and his whole family. Later Abraham gave God all the glory for the victory!

Remember this, when the enemy attacks your family, he is attacking God's family! Everything that Abraham had belonged to God including Abraham's family. Perhaps Lot wasn't the best person that ever lived, but he was Abraham's nephew and that was enough to get God's help for his salvation. God's covenant promises required Him to rescue Abraham's family members!

Lot went back to Sodom after his uncle rescued him. As we already mentioned, Sodom is known as one of the most wicked cities of all times. Maybe Lot didn't know that when he first chose to live there, but he certainly did after being there a while. Nonetheless, he still chose to go back with his family and live there again.

Just a side thought: If you make a mistake through a bad choice, you don't have to pitch your tent and live there forever! Lot should have just pulled up his tent stakes and gone back to Uncle Abraham or at least tried to find a better place to live. He could have made a new start somewhere else! Remember that if you ever find yourself in a wicked and unholy situation. Be smart enough to admit your mistake, get out of there and start over! This time ask the Lord for His advice and follow it!

Anyway - Later, the cities of Sodom and Gomorrah had become so wicked that God determined to judge and destroy them! I know this sounds unlike the God of love that we have been talking about, so let me say a few words about that before we continue with the story of Abraham and Lot.

Love and Judgment

First, God is love and He is good. He never changes which means He is always loving and always good. He is a Father to all

His family. He is a faithful covenant Partner. All people on earth are invited into His covenant and can become members of His family by grace through faith. ALL PEOPLE! But God is also the judge of the world and of those who reject His offer of grace. He's good but He's also the judge!

Secondly, all people are eternal spiritual beings. After their life on earth ends, they will live forever – either with God in heaven or eternally separated from God in hell. The people of Sodom and Gomorrah were wicked, unrepentant and rejected God. They raised their children to follow their wicked ways. This means that one generation after the other was being born, raised to live wickedly, to reject God and after death be eternally separated from God in hell.

It breaks God's heart when the wicked die and go to hell. The people of Sodom and Gomorrah were producing generations of people who would wind up in hell because of their wickedness. Judgment in this sense was mercy. It was the only way to stop this wicked, vicious cycle.

They certainly knew about Abraham and his covenant with the Most High God. It was Abraham who had rescued them. Although they knew that Abraham's God was the Most High God, they rejected Him and lived on in their wickedness. God had to put an end to it so that they wouldn't continue to populate hell. When God brings judgment there is always a redemptive aspect connected to it. He is always completely righteous in all His judgments.

Now back to the story.

GENESIS 18:17-21 *And the Lord said, "Shall I hide from Abraham what I am doing, since Abraham shall surely become a great and mighty nation, and all the nations of the earth shall be blessed in him? For I have known him, in order that he may command his children and his household after him, that they keep the way of the Lord, to do righteousness and justice, that the Lord may bring to*

*Abraham what He has spoken to him." And the Lord said,
"Because the outcry against Sodom and Gomorrah is great, and
because their sin is very grave, I will go down now and see
whether they have done altogether according to the outcry against
it that has come to Me; and if not, I will know."*

God told Abraham about His plans BECAUSE Abraham
was his covenant partner – AND BECAUSE Abraham's nephew
Lot was still living in Sodom. Abraham immediately began to
intercede for the people of Sodom and Gomorrah.

GENESIS 18:23-25 *And Abraham came near and said, "Would
You also destroy the righteous with the wicked? Suppose there
were fifty righteous within the city; would You also destroy the
place and not spare it for the fifty righteous that were in it? Far be
it from You to do such a thing as this, to slay the righteous with the
wicked, so that the righteous should be as the wicked; far be it
from You! Shall not the Judge of all the earth do right?"*

Abraham interceded because He had a covenant with
God. He was very bold in His prayer. We are also invited to come
boldly before the throne of grace! **(Hebrews 4:16)** Through his
prayer, he persuaded God to agree upon sparing the cities if He
could find 10 righteous people living there. I believe that if
Abraham had continued to intercede for them all the way down to
one righteous person, God would have spared the cities.

This story raises two questions:

1. Why did God tell Abraham about His plans to destroy
   Sodom and Gomorrah? He is the Judge of all the earth
   and has a right to do whatever He determines is best for
   the world. So, why tell Abraham?

2. Why did Abraham intercede for two cities that were
   undeniably two of the most wicked cities in all of history?
   They certainly deserved judgment and yet Abraham
   interceded for them. Why?

Both questions have one answer: LOT

Abraham was God's covenant partner and Lot was the nephew of God's covenant partner. Lot was in danger. God cares about you and your family. He even cares about your nephews! Abraham interceded because of Lot. I believe that God would have spared all of Sodom for the sake of Lot if Abraham had continued to intercede to that point.

Sodom and Gomorrah deserved judgment, but God would not destroy the cities without first telling Abraham. Moreover, He didn't destroy the cities until arrangements could be made to save and deliver Lot, the nephew of His covenant partner.

GENESIS 19:29 *And it came to pass, when God destroyed the cities of the plain, that **God remembered Abraham**, and sent Lot out of the midst of the overthrow, when he overthrew the cities in the which Lot dwelt.*

That's why God rescued Lord and his family from the terrible judgment that came upon the wicked city in which they dwelt. God remembered Abraham and the covenant.

Say it out loud:

"God saved Lot *and* his family!"

The only reason mentioned as to why God saved Lot is that "God remembered Abraham". He remembered His covenant with Abraham and the covenant included protection and salvation for every member of his family! Your family becomes God's responsibility because of the covenant.

I want to remind you that it had nothing to do with how good or bad Lot was. It wasn't dependent on Lot's righteousness but on God's covenant promise. And Lot should be very, very happy about that! We should be too!

If you know the story, you'll remember that God sent two

angels to investigate the situation in Sodom as well as to deliver Lot. The two angels appeared as men. When they entered the city, they went to Lot's house. All the men of the city gathered around the house and demanded that Lot-send the men (angels) out to them, so that they could have sex with them.

To his credit, Lot refused to do it but to his shame he offered them his daughters instead.

GENESIS 19:7-8 *and (Lot) said, "Please, my brethren, do not do so wickedly! See now, I have two daughters who have not known a man; please, let me bring them out to you, and you may do to them as you wish; only do nothing to these men, since this is the reason they have come under the shadow of my roof."*

What? Lot was not a very good father! He was living a life of compromise and he knew it. He was about to give his daughters to the wicked men of Sodom to be sexually abused – BUT THANK GOD – the angels wouldn't allow it! They protected him and his family. God rescued Lot – but He rescued him for one reason and one reason only. It wasn't because he was deserved it. It was because his uncle Abraham had a covenant with God and that covenant included promises, provision and protection for his whole family – including nephews.

God placed a special priority on Lot's salvation because of Abraham. God also places a priority on the salvation of your family members because of you. You are in covenant with God through the precious blood of Jesus. Because of the covenant, your family members are priority to God.

I believe that if God wants to save our nephews, He wants to save our nieces also. If He wants to save our nieces, then He surely wants to save our brothers and sisters. If He wants to save our brothers and sisters, then surely He wants to save our parents too. If parents, then grandparents, if grandparents, then grandchildren and so on and so forth. God is a God of families.

When He saved Noah from the great flood,

He saved Noah and his family

including his daughters-in-law!

When He made covenant with Abraham,

it included Abraham and his whole family

for generations to come.

When God made a covenant with King David,

It included David's family forever!

God has always desired to save households and families

and God never changes.

The promise to the Philippian jailer was not just some new thing that Paul came up with. It was a revelation of the heart of God for every family because of the New Covenant sealed with the precious blood of Jesus Christ.

Some think that the covenant God made with Abraham has nothing to do with us today because it is the Old Covenant. It is indeed the Old Covenant, but we have a covenant too! The New Covenant is a better covenant based upon better promises. **(Hebrews 8:6)** It is better because it includes every blessing of the Old Covenant PLUS! For example, a one hundred dollar bill is better than a ten-dollar bill because it has all the ten dollars PLUS!

Not only that, but the blessings that God promised to Abraham belong to everyone who believes in Jesus Christ today! Look at the following scriptures and see what belongs to you.

GALATIANS 3:7 *Therefore know that only those who are of faith are sons of Abraham. And the Scripture, foreseeing that God would justify the Gentiles by faith, preached the gospel to Abraham beforehand, saying, "In you all the nations shall be blessed." So then those who are of faith are blessed with believing*

Abraham.

- **You are blessed!**

GALATIANS 3:13-14 *Christ has redeemed us from the curse of the law, having become a curse for us (for it is written, "Cursed is everyone who hangs on a tree"), that the blessing of Abraham might come upon the Gentiles in Christ Jesus, that we might receive the promise of the Spirit through faith.*

- **God's promises to Abraham belong to you!**

GALATIANS 3:29 *And if you are Christ's, then you are Abraham's seed, and heirs according to the promise.*

- **We are Abraham's offspring and heirs!**

In Christ, we are heirs and recipients of the promises that God made to Abraham. God preached the gospel to Abraham. His covenant with Abraham was the forerunner of the New Covenant. The Abrahamic covenant could not give the new birth or the baptism with the Holy Spirit, but it has many blessings that apply to us today.

The blessing of Abraham comes upon every believer in Jesus Christ. Find out what God promised Abraham and remember that you are his heir!

We have a new and better covenant!

The promises made to Abraham belong to us

PLUS the new birth,

PLUS the baptism with the Holy Spirit,

PLUS every spiritual blessing!

The blood covenant that God made with Abraham saved Abraham, his immediate family, his nephew Lot and Lot's family too. It also included all of his descendants for generations to come. Once again, we have a new and better covenant. How much more will the New Covenant signed and sealed with the blood of Jesus Christ save our whole family!

It is God's will to save your family members. It is a covenant right. You can stand steadfastly on the promise in **ACTS 16:31**, *"Believe on the Lord Jesus Christ and you'll be saved and your house."* God wants your family saved because you are in covenant with Him.

Of course, for your family members to be saved they will have to receive Jesus Christ as their Lord. This is a free-will decision that they must make, and God will not override their free will. However, through your prayers, God can work on their will and bring them to the point of decision. He can be very persuasive. The decision remains theirs to make but we can help them.

How can we help them? Read on. In the following pages, you will see how to act upon your covenant rights through prayer. This is not some empty formula or dead religious work designed to keep you busy. It is a practical approach to praying your family members into the kingdom of God. It works! It has worked for thousands of people worldwide and it will work for you. You and your whole house shall be saved!

USE YOUR AUTHORITY

2 CORINTHIANS 4:3-4 But even if our gospel is veiled, it is veiled to those who are perishing, whose minds the god of this age has blinded, who do not believe, lest the light of the gospel of the glory of Christ, who is the image of God, should shine on them.

The enemy of God and humanity is blinding the minds of those who do not believe the good news of Jesus. Therefore, they can't understand why we are so excited about Jesus. Maybe they think that we are religiously inclined or that we need some kind of emotional or mental crutch to get by in life. We know better, because we have been born again. We see things, hear things and know things that they can't see, hear and know! Their spiritual senses have been dulled and blinded.

Jesus told Nicodemus, *"Most assuredly, I say to you, unless one is born again, he cannot see the kingdom of God."* (**John 3:3**) People who have not been born again cannot see the kingdom of God. They cannot understand spiritual things. Paul put it this way, *"The natural man does not receive the things of the Spirit of God, for they are foolishness to him; nor can he know them, because they are spiritually discerned."* (**1 Corinthians 2:14**) They cannot understand spiritual things because the "god" of this world (satan) has blinded them.

Right now, as you read this book, the enemy is working against your yet to be saved family members. They may not even realize it, but it is true. Those who are not born again are under the power of the devil. I know it sounds extreme but it's true. As Christians, we know this because we were in the same condition before we were saved. More importantly, we know it because the Bible says so.

EPHESIANS 2:1-3 *And you He made alive, who were dead in trespasses and sins, in which you once walked according to the course of this world, according to the prince of the power of the air, the spirit who now works in the sons of disobedience, among whom also we all once conducted ourselves in the lusts of our flesh, fulfilling the desires of the flesh and of the mind, and were by nature children of wrath, just as the others.*

We were dead in sins. We know what it was like. Paul says that everyone who is still in that condition is living according to the prince of the power of the air, also known as the devil. Many of them don't even believe in the devil. His "nonexistence" is one of his greatest lies. People believe they are in control and that they are just doing what they want to do. They can quit smoking, drinking, watching pornography, fornicating, cussing any time they want – at least that's what they say. I know one man who said, "Quitting smoking is the easiest thing to do in the whole world! I've already quit at least 100 times."

Even "nice" sinners and "good" sinners are under the power of the enemy. Their unbelief is not just a matter of rational thinking, as they would like us to believe. Their unbelief is the result of believing the lies of the enemy and rejecting the truth of God.

So, what can we do about that?

Pray! In the next pages, you are going to learn how to pray for your yet to be saved family members. The principles are applicable to anyone who is not yet saved, but in this book, we are focusing on our families.

Through prayer – among other things – we can exercise our God given authority. We can forbid and counteract the works of the enemy and pave the way for God's plans and purpose. Before Jesus ascended into Heaven, He spoke to His disciples and commissioned them to preach the gospel and make disciples of all nations and people groups. He also gave them power and authority to do the job.

MARK 16:15-18 *And He said to them, "Go into all the world and preach the gospel to every creature. He who believes and is baptized will be saved; but he who does not believe will be condemned. And these signs will follow those who believe: In My name they will cast out demons; they will speak with new tongues; they will take up serpents; and if they drink anything deadly, it will by no means hurt them; they will lay hands on the sick, and they will recover."*

We call this the Great Commission because of how great our Savior is. It's great because of how big the job is. It's great because of how great the message is. It's also great because of the great power and authority that Jesus gave us. The Great Commission was not just for the apostles. It is for all believers of all times until Jesus returns. Correspondingly, the power and authority that Jesus gave believers back then, is also for all believers of all times until He returns.

Jesus said, *"These signs shall follow those who believe".* He didn't say, *"These signs will follow the apostles."*

Make sure that you build your faith on the Bible and on what Jesus said. Don't let theologians – the ones who contradict what Jesus said – influence what you believe. Sadly, the traditions of man and the excuses of dead religion have destroyed the faith of many people.

You have power and authority over the "god of this world", who is blinding the minds of your yet to be saved loved ones! The first sign that Jesus said would follow believers is that they would cast out demons in His name. One preacher said, "Today most churches don't believe in casting out demons, they believe in casting out preachers who cast out demons!" ☺

Again, build your faith on what the Bible says! This sign is not for a special category of Christians. It belongs to every believer through the name of Jesus Christ.

We find the Great Commission in the gospel of Matthew as well. It begins with these words:

MATTHEW 28:18-19 *And Jesus came and spoke to them, saying, "All authority has been given to Me in heaven and on earth. Go therefore and make disciples of all the nations"*

Jesus recovered the authority that God had given to Adam and Eve in the Garden of Eden. God gave humanity power and authority to reign over the earth and everything in it. When Adam and Eve sinned, they transferred this authority to the enemy.

When they submitted to the enemy, all that they were and all that they had came under his power. In that very moment, the devil started his hideous reign of sin and death. As Paul said, he became the "god of this world". Jesus referred to the devil as "the ruler of this world" three times. **(John 12:32, 14:30, 16:11)** This foul being is blinding the minds of those who do not believe.

We can do something about it! Jesus recovered humanity's lost authority! He said, *"All authority in Heaven and earth has been given to me".* If Jesus has "all" authority, that means that the enemy has NO authority! Jesus immediately transferred this authority to us in the Great Commission! He said, "You go – you preach the gospel, you make disciples, you cast out demons, and you heal the sick in My name!" He gave us authority to act in His name!

In the name of Jesus, we can exercise authority over the enemy who is blinding our loved ones. We can issue commands and the "god of this world" must obey us in the wonderful name that is above all names!

Binding and Loosing

MATTHEW 18:18-20 *Assuredly, I say to you, whatever you bind on earth will be bound in heaven, and whatever you loose on earth will be loosed in heaven. Again I say to you that if two of you agree on earth concerning anything that they ask, it will be done for them by My Father in heaven. For where two or three are gathered together in My name, I am there in the midst of them.*

This verse repeats in part what Jesus said to Peter in **Matthew 16:18**. Theologians have various views about what the words "binding and loosing" mean. Some think it refers to a special authority given to Peter to open the door of the Gospel to the Jews and later to the Gentiles. Others say that Jesus gave the apostles special authority to exercise discipline in the church. The previous context does refer to discipline so that does make sense. Still others interpret this to apply directly to the teaching ministry of the apostles. "Binding and loosing" was a familiar phrase used by Jewish Rabbis to differentiate between teachings that were accepted and teachings that were rejected.

Regardless of how we understand this passage of Scripture, it contains several truths that are applicable to each one of us.

This authority was delivered to the whole church. In the previous verse **(Matthew 18:17)** Jesus said, "If he (the disobedient one) refuses to hear *the church*, let him be to you like a heathen and a tax collector." Therefore, the authority to bind and to loose was given to the whole church. This agrees with what we already read about concerning the authority to cast out demons. It belongs to every believer. It belongs to the whole church!

Secondly, we know that in **Matthew 18:18**, Jesus is speaking of "binding and loosing" in the context of prayer. In **verse 19** He says, "Again I say unto you" which directly connects verse

19 to verse 18. In other words, Jesus said, "Here's another way to say what I just said in verse 18". In verse 19, Jesus says that when we agree in prayer ON EARTH, it will be done for us by our Father IN HEAVEN. The binding and loosing that Jesus was referring to is connected to prayer. What we bind and loose ON EARTH is bound and loosed IN HEAVEN. What we ask for in agreement ON EARTH will be done for us by our Father IN HEAVEN.

Going a step further, the words "binding and loosing" mean "things we prohibit and things we permit". Many translations make this point clear.

MATTHEW 18:18 *I tell you this: Whatever you prohibit on earth is prohibited in heaven, and whatever you allow on earth is allowed in heaven.* **NLT**

Whatever we prohibit will be prohibited.

Whatever we allow will be allowed.

This statement agrees with what the Bible says about humanity possessing free will and the ability to determine their own destiny. Our choices determine our destiny. There are those who believe that free will is an illusion and that we have no ability to choose. They think that God directly causes everything that happens. Thank God that such claims are untrue. If God causes everything that happens, then God would be the biggest sinner of all times. Jesus said:

MATTHEW 18:6 *But if you cause one of these little ones who trusts in me to fall into sin, it would be better for you to have a large millstone tied around your neck and be drowned in the depths of the sea.*

If God causes everything that happens, then He must be causing people to sin because they are certainly doing a lot of it. No, that's nonsense! He told Adam not to eat the fruit of the tree of the knowledge of good and evil because He knew that if he did,

Adam would die. He didn't want him to do it. He didn't want Adam to die. It wasn't His will for mankind to sin. God is not schizophrenic. Some theologians may be schizophrenic, but God is not. People have a free will and God allows us to choose.

God also knows all things. He knows what everyone will choose to do, but that doesn't mean that He made the choice for them! There is a big difference between God knowing what will happen and God causing those things to happen.

Many people don't realize that God doesn't *only* exist in eternity and outside of His creation. He is eternal but He also is ever present and all-knowing. He sees each moment and experiences each moment with us in real time. Because He knows all things, He can inspire us, encourage us and make a way for us but we still have to choose to walk in the way that He makes for us.

I really don't want to spend a lot of time on this, but it is important. So many people think that their life is a script that God wrote before they were born and that there's nothing that they can do to change it. This is simply not the case. If it was, then how could God condemn people for doing what He, as a sovereign, almighty Being, forced them to do? That would be unjust, and God is not unjust. Here are some thoughts that support the biblical fact that we all have a free will and can make choices that determine our destiny.

God told Adam, "Don't eat from the tree of the knowledge of good and evil". **(Genesis 2:17)** If God made Adam sin, then He forced Adam to sin against His own commandment. How crazy would that be? That would be very crazy, and God is not crazy!

Moses told the Israelites to "choose life". **(Deuteronomy 30:19)** If they couldn't choose, then this was nothing more than deceptive, empty words. But Moses spoke the word of God and God is not a deceiver. To be able to choose you must have a free will.

Jesus called the disciples to follow Him. If they couldn't choose to follow Him, then this was just a charade. If He was causing or forcing them to follow, then they weren't following, they were being driven.

Jesus told us time and time again, to pray and to ask things of the Father. If God causes and preordains everything that happens, then prayer would be a farce and asking a waste of time. Why tell us to ask, if He's going to do what He wants to do anyway?

Every conditional promise that God made would be fraudulent if you can't make choices. For example, in **JOHN 15:7** Jesus said, *"If you abide in Me, and My words abide in you, you will ask what you desire, and it shall be done for you."* If you can't choose to abide in Christ, this promise is meaningless. Even the premise of what Jesus promises would be deception. *"If you ask what you desire, it will be done."* If God causes everything, then you have no desires of your own, which would make this promise and the premise of the promise no more than deception and fraud.

God is no deceiver.

Jesus is no deceiver.

The Bible is not deceptive.

Like I said, I don't want to dwell too long on the topic of God's sovereignty and humanity's free will but "binding and loosing" or "forbidding and permitting" is only possible if we have a free will.

Listen carefully: **YOU DON'T HAVE TO LET THE DEVIL TAKE YOUR FAMILY TO HELL! YOU CAN CHOOSE TO DO SOMETHING ABOUT IT.**

In God's foreknowledge, He knows all things. He wants to help us, provide for us, protect us and He has good plans for us, but we must choose His plans.

If everyone is experiencing God's perfect will for their lives right now, then every child starving to death, every woman who was raped, every city and neighborhood that was bombed in war was God's will. But these things are NOT His will.

What God permits and what He causes are two different things.

What He wills and what He allows are also two different things.

He allows what we allow.

He forbids what we forbid.

Still, people continually accuse God. They say, "If God knew that all these things were going to happen, then it's His fault for creating us in the first place." The truth is that God is **responsible** for everything that ever happened but everything that happened is not His **fault.** He is responsible because He is the One who pushed the "start button" in the beginning. If He didn't begin the beginning, nothing that happened afterward would have happened. BUT – there is a huge difference between responsibility and fault.

God is not guilty of the actions of humanity, but He is responsible for them. He knew what they would do but He never forced them to do it. And in His IMPOSSIBLE TO DESCRIBE BIGNESS, He already took complete responsibility for everything that ever happened. On the cross, He took responsibility and paid for every sin ever committed by a human being.

Those who accuse God and want to put the blame on Him, came too late. He already took full responsibility for every horrible thing that ever happened. He said, "Put the blame on Me. I will pay your debt." He wasn't guilty of sin. He didn't force people to sin. But He took the responsibility for it as Creator and God.

When Jesus died on the cross, He assumed our place and took the judgment that we deserved because of our sinful, disobedient choices.

This is the good news.

Jesus took our guilt and shame.

God paid our penalty in full!

If we believe on and receive Jesus,

there is nothing left for us to pay.

His sacrificial death on the cross, was more than enough to wash away all our sins and give us eternal life!

We chose sin – He chose righteousness. He took our place and received what we deserved. By faith, He gives us His place at the right hand of God, and we receive eternal blessings that we didn't deserve.

I could go on and on. Volumes have been written about God's sovereignty and man's free will, but that's enough for now. Let's get back to the point at hand.

You can bind the devil's plans and loose the plans of God on earth through prayer! In other words, you can make decisions about what you allow and what you prohibit in your life. Jesus gave us authority over satan and the forces of darkness. We are not under their power, and we do not have to allow them to dictate to us what will happen in our lives or in the lives of our families. We can bind the devil. We can prohibit him from working in our families!

We read that one of the devil's activities is blinding the minds of those who do not believe – including our yet to be saved family members. You can bind the enemy and break his power over their lives. You can command him in the name of Jesus Christ to take his blinders off their minds. Jesus clearly gave us the authority to do something against the works of the devil in our lives and in the lives of our families.

Jesus is our example of a life of victory over the powers of the enemy. He repeatedly set people free from the bondage of satan. In His mission statement in Luke chapter 4, Jesus read from Isaiah 61.

LUKE 4:17-18 *And He was handed the book of the prophet Isaiah. And when He had opened the book, He found the place where it was written: "The Spirit of the Lord is upon Me, because He has anointed Me to preach the gospel to the poor; He has sent Me to heal the brokenhearted, to proclaim liberty to the captives and recovery of sight to the blind, to set at liberty those who are oppressed.*

Jesus said that His followers (a.k.a. believers) would do the same works and greater works than He did.

JOHN 14:12 *Most assuredly, I say to you, he who believes in Me, the works that I do he will do also; and greater works than these he will do, because I go to My Father.*

He came to set captives free, and we are called to set the captives free. Jesus did this in various ways but one of the most common ways He did this was by simply commanding the devil to leave people.

MARK 1:23 *Now there was a man in their synagogue with an unclean spirit. And he cried out, saying, "Let us alone! What have we to do with You, Jesus of Nazareth? Did You come to destroy us? I know who You are – the Holy One of God!" But Jesus rebuked him, saying, "Be quiet, and come out of him!"*

He told unclean and evil spirits to leave people. Many times, He prefaced these words with, "Be quiet" or "shut up". The devil has a big mouth and wants to talk and try to deceive people. Tell him to shut up and leave in the name of Jesus! Bind the enemy and command him to take his blinders off your family! You have authority over him in the name of Jesus.

You don't have to be directly in the presence of the person who is being influenced by the enemy, to exercise authority over the evil spirits that are blinding them. There is no distance in the realm or dimension of the spirit. We can see this truth in several scriptures in the New Testament. For example, Paul said that we are seated with Christ in the heavenly places.

EPHESIANS 2:6 *And God raised us up with Christ and seated us with him in the heavenly realms in Christ Jesus*

This is not something that will happen later. This is a present reality. Regardless of where you are right now in this world physically, you are also seated with Christ in the heavenly places. It has been said that we can only be in one place at a time, but Paul said something different. We are here on earth, but we are also seated with Christ in Heaven at the right hand of God. This is the place where all power and authority dwells. This shows us that there is no distance, as we understand it, in the realm of the spirit.

Paul was in a Roman prison when he wrote his letter to the Colossians. In it he said, "For though I am absent in the flesh, yet I am with you in spirit, rejoicing to see your good order and the steadfastness of your faith in Christ.". **(Colossians 2:5)** He was in prison, but he was also in Colossae – in the spirit. In the spirit, he was able to see and know things that were happening in Colossae. As I said, you can be in more than one place at one time! This is a powerful truth for our prayer lives.

It can also be a big help for the parents of teenagers! ☺

Speaking along these lines Jesus said, *"At that day you will know that I am in My Father, and you in Me, and I in you."* **(John 14:20)** This means that wherever you are right now, you are also right there where Jesus is. He is at the right hand of the Father, but He is also right here with me. He is right there with you, and I am right there with you in Him.

Distance in the realm of the spirit is apparently different than distance in our three-dimensional world. Human beings are multi-dimensional beings. We are beings of time and space but

61

also beings of the spiritual dimension. No matter where your yet to be saved loved one lives are, you can command the devil to turn them loose and let them go in the name of Jesus. You are there in the realm of the spirit and have authority in the name of Jesus!

1 JOHN 3:8b *For this purpose the Son of God was manifested, that he might destroy the works of the devil.*

Jesus has already broken the power of the enemy and destroyed his works, but we must enforce these truths here on earth. When Jesus arose from the dead He said, *"All authority in heaven and earth is given unto Me!"* And then He gave it to us! The devil has no authority to do what he is doing except the authority that people give him. We can break that power by the true authority that is recognized by God himself! What we bind on earth is bound in heaven!

Think about this: When Jesus shed His blood on the cross, He paid to redeem all of humanity. This means He purchased all people with His blood. In other words, the devil has no legal right to oppress or bind any human being. Many people don't know or believe these things. Many people willingly submit to the enemy. This, however, does not change the fact that Jesus paid for their deliverance and freedom! The victory is already won. As followers of Jesus, we are the occupational troops. We are called to enforce the victory of Jesus. Wherever we see the enemy still asserting influence and holding people captive, we are to set them free!

Command the devil to let them go in the name of our victorious King Jesus!

The victory of Jesus belongs to us as Christians, but we must lay hold of that victory and partake of its benefits. We must believe and receive. We must exercise faith and take what He has provided. In the same way, we must also use the authority He has entrusted to us. The devil is already defeated but we must enforce that defeat.

We have authority to resist the devil and work against his plans and schemes.

JAMES 4:7 *Therefore submit to God. Resist the devil and he will flee from you.*

In the Greek, which is the original language of the New Testament, the word translated as "resist" is "anthistemi". Of course, it means to resist but it also means to withstand or to set oneself against. In the Louw und Nida Greek-English Lexicon, "anthistemi" is defined as *"to resist by actively opposing pressure or power. In a number of languages, one may appropriately translate 'to resist' in a number of contexts as 'to fight back against' or 'to oppose in return.'"* (from Greek-English Lexicon Based on Semantic Domain. Copyright © 1988 United Bible Societies, New York. Used by permission.)

The enemy is fighting against your lost loved ones. He is fighting against the salvation of your family. He is seeking to steal, kill and destroy. But we can rise in the name of Jesus and fight back! He has no legal right to do what he is doing. We, on the other hand, have the legal right to bind him, resist him, withstand him and fight back. Our authority is from God. God stands behind this authority and will back up our words and actions when they are done in faith and in the name of Jesus!

The apostle Paul also told us to do something against the works of the enemy.

EPHESIANS 4:27 *Give no place to the devil.*

If the devil has a place in our lives, it is because we have given it to him. Don't allow him a place in your life or in that of your family. Don't let him take your yet to be saved loved ones to hell! Break his power over their lives.

Just to clarify, I am not saying that every unbeliever who is blinded by the devil is demon possessed. They aren't. But they are under his influence. They can still choose to do right and be nice and most of them probably do, most of the time. However, when we are talking about their spiritual nature, they are separated from God and under the authority of darkness.

You don't necessarily have to cast a demon out of them. You just have to command the devil to loose them and let them go. The devil has no legal right to take your family to hell. If you consistently exercise your authority, he will have to let them go!

I want to remind you that we are talking about prayer. Prayer is more than asking God to do things. Prayer is worshipping God, fellowshipping with God, giving thanks to God, talking to God and bringing our requests to God – but it is also binding and loosing. In the authority of the name of Jesus, we forbid and permit things on earth. There are times to ask God to do things for you and there are times to command or demand things to happen in the authority of Jesus' name!

JOHN 14:14 *If you ask anything in My name, I will do it.*

The Greek word used in this verse for "ask" is "aiteo" and it means, "to ask for with urgency, even to the point of demanding". (Greek-English Lexicon Based on Semantic Domain. Copyright © 1988 United Bible Societies, New York. Used by permission.) In this case, we are not demanding anything of Jesus. We are using His name to demand and command sickness or evil spirits to leave people. He said that if we demand these things in His name, He will do it. In other words, the power that is in His name will carry out the thing requested or demanded. Here are few examples of this:

ACTS 3:6 *Then Peter said, "Silver and gold I do not have, but what I do have I give you: In the name of Jesus Christ of Nazareth, rise up and walk."*

Peter didn't pray for the man. He commanded him to rise and walk in the name of Jesus! He wasn't commanding Jesus to do anything. He commanded the man. Rise and be healed in the name of Jesus. There is power in the name of Jesus!

When Peter used the name of Jesus, Jesus was there with him and Jesus healed the man! How was Jesus there? He was there in His Name! Here's another example:

Acts 16:18 *But Paul, greatly annoyed, turned and said to the spirit, "I command you in the name of Jesus Christ to come out of her." And he came out that very hour.*

Paul didn't pray or ask to God to make the demon leave the woman. He commanded or demanded that the spirit leave her in the name of Jesus! Demons must obey us when we command them in the name of Jesus! When Paul commanded the spirit to leave in the name of Jesus, Jesus was there, and Jesus set the woman free! Again, how was Jesus there? He was there in His name!

We can exercise this same authority in our prayer closet. We demand and command the enemy to remove his blinders in the name of Jesus! Jesus is there and Jesus backs up what we say. HEAVEN backs up what we say ON EARTH in Jesus' name!

Remember the context of "binding and loosing".

Matthew 18:18-20 *Assuredly, I say to you, whatever you bind on earth will be bound in heaven, and whatever you loose on earth will be loosed in heaven. Again I say to you that if two of you agree on earth concerning anything that they ask, it will be done for them by My Father in heaven. For where two or three are gathered together in My name, I am there in the midst of them.*

In His name, we bind and loose things on earth and they are bound and loosed in heaven! In verse 19, Jesus said that this is referring to prayer. Then He says, *"Where two or three are gathered together IN MY NAME, I am there in their midst"*. He is there when we are binding and commanding evil spirits in His name. We are not demanding anything of Jesus, but we are forbidding demons from blinding and influencing our families. Jesus – Who is there with us – IN HIS NAME – enforces it. We are working together with Him Who is present in His wonderful, matchless name!

Command the devil to take his hands off your family in the Name of Jesus!

Revelation versus Information

Kenneth E. Hagin, told the following story in his great book entitled, "The Believer's Authority". *(I highly recommend that you buy it and read it.)* He said that one day while meditating on the scriptures he received a mighty revelation of the believer's authority and power in the name of Jesus. His brother Dub was the so-called "black sheep" of the family. No one in the family thought he would ever be saved. While this revelation of the believer's authority was burning brightly in his heart he stood to his feet and boldly commanded, "Devil, take your hand off my brother's life in the name of the Lord Jesus Christ. I claim his soul for the kingdom of God. Father God, I thank you for his salvation right now in Jesus' name!"

A few days later the devil tried to get him into doubt and unbelief about it. He said, "You don't really think your brother will get saved, do you?" He answered and said, "No, I don't think he'll get saved. I never thought he would get saved and I don't think it now. I KNOW HE'LL GET SAVED because I broke your power over his life in Jesus' name and claimed his salvation by faith!" To make the long story short, two weeks later his brother Dub was born again!

This is the difference between revelation knowledge and mere information. There is a great difference between doing the steps in a formula because someone told you about it and really knowing and believing something in your heart. The Word of God does not work for us just because we have a certain formula. It works for us when it is real in our hearts. Faith is of the heart. We must be convinced with all our heart that the authority Jesus gave to us will also work for us. Meditate on these things until the light of that revelation dawns on your heart. The devil must obey you when you use the mighty name of Jesus!

As a believer, you are the authorized one in your family. It is up to you to command the enemy to take his hands off your loved ones in the name of Jesus. In addition, you may have noticed that the devil has a poor memory. This is probably because Jesus crushed his head when He arose from the dead! ☺ You may have to remind him time and again that your family is off limits to him. Remind him and remind yourself of his total defeat and of God's trustworthy promise. Believe on the Lord Jesus Christ and you will be saved and your whole family!

Don't Let the Devil Take Your Family to Hell

Your family members still have a free will. Even though we can break the devil's blinding power over them they can still consciously or unconsciously open the door to him again. You will have to stay aggressive. Don't give him an inch. Don't be overly "devil and demon conscious" but at the same time don't shut your eyes and allow him to destroy your family.

2 CORINTHIANS 2:11 *Lest Satan should get an advantage of us: for we are not ignorant of his devices.*

When Paul said that we are not ignorant of satan's devices, he wasn't saying that we should be overly concerned with the devil, but we shouldn't close our eyes and pretend he's not there either. We know that he is continually looking for those he can destroy and devour.

1 PETER 5:8 *Be sober, be vigilant; because your adversary the devil walks about like a roaring lion, seeking whom he may devour.*

He is looking for opportunities, but we refuse to give him any. He is seeking to devour people. Don't allow him to devour you or your family. He is looking for somebody to chew up and swallow but if we exercise our blood bought authority in the name of Jesus, he will not be able to devour us nor our families.

Fight for your Family

The story of how Nehemiah and the Israelites rebuilt the wall in Jerusalem after returning from captivity in Babylon provides us with some very wise counsel. They rebuilt the wall in just 52 days. There's so much to learn from this true story but one of the smartest things Nehemiah did was to assign people to build the part of the wall that directly affected them and their family. In other words, he commissioned them to build the parts of the wall right where they lived!

NEHEMIAH 3:23 *After him Benjamin and Hasshub made repairs opposite their house. After them Azariah the son of Maaseiah, the son of Ananiah, made repairs by his house.*

NEHEMIAH 3:28-30 *Beyond the Horse Gate the priests made repairs, each in front of his own house. After them Zadok the son of Immer made repairs in front of his own house. After him Shemaiah the son of Shechaniah, the keeper of the East Gate, made repairs. After him Hananiah the son of Shelemiah, and Hanun, the sixth son of Zalaph, repaired another section. After him Meshullam the son of Berechiah made repairs in front of his dwelling.*

These people had a personal stake in rebuilding the wall and making sure that it was sturdy and secure! The safety of their family was at stake. They were highly motivated to build a very strong wall.

At one point, enemies came and tried to distract and confuse them. They wanted to make them to stop building. They mocked the people and mocked the wall they were building. They said, *"That stone wall would collapse if even a fox walked along the top of it!" (Nehemiah 4,3)*

They secretly devised a plan to attack the builders and destroy the wall. Listen to what Nehemiah did and said:

NEHEMIAH 4:13-14 *Therefore I positioned men behind the lower* *parts of the wall, at the openings; and I set the people according to their families, with their swords, their spears, and their bows. And I looked, and arose and said to the nobles, to the leaders, and to the rest of the people, "Do not be afraid of them. Remember the Lord, great and awesome, and fight for your brethren, your sons, your daughters, your wives, and your houses."*

He stationed people together according to their families and told them to fight! Fight for your family! This should be our battle cry today! There is a war against the family. There is an enemy that wants to distract and confuse us. He wants to steal, kill, destroy and take our families to hell! Fight for your family!

Don't be afraid of the enemy. His defenses are gone. He is weaponless. All that he has is a big mouth full of lies. Stand up! Take your place in front of your family. When the enemy comes, take your sword and chase him off. The sword of the spirit is the word of God! It is the word that you believe and proclaim! Speak it over your family! Speak protection, freedom and salvation over them! There is a fight to be fought but it is a fight that Jesus already won! Stand in your victory! Put the enemy to flight with the mighty name of Jesus! Fight the good fight of faith for your family.

We Wrestle Not Against Flesh and Blood

EPHESIANS 6:12 *For we do not wrestle against flesh and blood, but against principalities, against powers, against the rulers of the darkness of this age, against spiritual hosts of wickedness in the heavenly places.*

We need to realize that there are evil spirits working behind the scenes in the lives of unsaved people that will have to be bound. We are not fighting against flesh and blood but there are spiritual forces trying to hinder our prayers and faith in God. Exercising our authority boldly in faith is the way to victory.

It could be that some of your family members are antagonistic and resisting the gospel! I know that they can say hurtful and offensive things but remember that the enemy has blinded them. Forgive them for they know not what they do! Don't be angry with them. Fight *for* them not *against* them! ☺

Maybe they are alcoholics, drug addicts or bound by sexual perversion. Don't forget that the battle is not just mental or physical. There are dark forces that hate God and hate you who are working against them. Don't wrestle against their addictions and perversions in the flesh. Use your spiritual authority in Jesus!

One evening, I was preaching in a Catholic Church in Austria. I preached the gospel and then gave an invitation for people to receive Jesus Christ as their Lord and Savior! About twenty people raised their hands and came forward to give their lives to Jesus. Afterward we prayed for the sick. God did some wonderful miracles that night.

At the very end of the service, we invited anyone who needed prayer to come forward. One lady came to the front and told me that her husband had been an alcoholic for many years and was very abusive. He was continually angry and often screamed and cussed at her. He especially hated the fact that she visited our church in Wels. Looking into her eyes, I saw a woman who had been deeply hurt. She was desperate and asked me to pray for their marriage.

LISTEN VERY CAREFULLY: I took about two minutes and explained to her the authority that Jesus has given us. I explained that there are evil spirits blinding and influencing people and that this was most likely the case with her husband. I told her to take authority over those dark forces and to break their power over her husband's life in Jesus' name.

It took about two minutes.

It wasn't any more than that.

Two minutes can be powerful!

I prayed for her and her husband that evening, but I also explained to her that she would have to exercise her authority as a Christian on a continual basis. I told her, "Command the enemy to take his hands off your husband in Jesus' name". I told her not to do it in his presence because that would most likely provoke his carnal and aggressive personality. Our warfare is a spiritual warfare.

I said, "When he's drunk, angry and being unreasonable, go into the next room and quietly say, 'devil, take your hands off my husband right now! You have no right and no authority here. I command you to go in the name of Jesus!'"

I asked her, "Can you do that? Will you do that?" She assured me that she could and that she would.

About a week later, she came to our church and was very excited. She shouted, "Pastor Fred, Pastor Fred! It's a miracle! It's a miracle! My husband is like a different man. I did what you said and now my husband is a changed person. He quit drinking and told me that I can come to church! He even said he wants to come to church with me!"

Miracle of miracles! He really did come to church! The very next week he came, gave his life to Jesus and was totally set free! His name was Karl. Several years ago, he went home to be with the Lord but from the day he was saved until he went home, he never drank another drop of alcohol! He loved his wife and family and treated them far better than he had ever done in his life. He wasn't perfect but he was radically changed and believed in Jesus until the day he went home. God's Word works!

Don't let the devil to take your loved ones to hell. Bind his workings and break his power over your family members so that the light of the glorious gospel of Jesus can shine into their hearts.

LET IT SHINE

A prophet is not without honor except in his own house

MARK 6:1-4 *Then He went out from there and came to His own country, and His disciples followed Him. And when the Sabbath had come, He began to teach in the synagogue. And many hearing Him were astonished, saying, "Where did this Man get these things? And what wisdom is this which is given to Him, that such mighty works are performed by His hands! Is this not the carpenter, the Son of Mary, and brother of James, Joses, Judas, and Simon? And are not His sisters here with us?" So they were offended at Him. But Jesus said to them, "A prophet is not without honor except in his own country, among his own relatives, and in his own house."*

Can you relate to this story? I know I can! I got born again and just had to tell everyone about Jesus. I was so thankful I couldn't hold back! Well, okay, I didn't want to hold back! I just kind of exploded on people! I started with my own family and friends. I think everyone does this and it's a good thing to make our stand for Jesus known.

When God saves us and changes our life, we want everyone to know about the love and joy we've found! But it wasn't long before I found out that what Jesus said here is true. *"A prophet is not without honor, except in his own country, and among his own kin, and in his own house."* Note that He specifically mentions family and those in your own household!

Sometimes the biggest resistance you'll receive will come from your yet to be saved family members. They can be just like the people in Jesus' hometown of Nazareth. The only difference is that they couldn't accuse Jesus of previously living a messed-up life. He was, is and remains perfect in every way. We weren't and still aren't.

The people closest to us know us. At least they know who we were and what we used to do! They saw how we lived in the past. They might say things like, "You're no better than me! I know what kind of person you were. Do you think you are holier than everyone else? You grew up here. I know all the mistakes you made and now you want to tell me what to believe? Who do you think you are? Don't tell me how to live my life!"

Some of my best friends told me, "You were always extreme. You're just going through your next weird phase. You need to be deprogrammed!" How true it is that a prophet is (usually) not accepted in his own house! There may be exceptions, but this is generally the case.

Don't Just Preach it – Live it.

What can we do about it? When it comes to your family, my advice is: Don't just preach it, make sure you live it!

A quote, falsely attributed to Francis of Assisi, says, "Preach the gospel at all times and use words when necessary." Although I don't totally agree with this saying – because people have to hear the gospel, believe it and receive Christ to be saved – it still might be better in our immediate family to preach less and shine more. In other words, let them see how wonderful Jesus is by living for Him in a loving and God honoring way.

I am not saying that we shouldn't talk to them about Jesus but sometimes being too preachy to our family members can do more harm than good. It can lead to arguments, hurts and words spoken that never should have been spoken. Some relatives might even begin to avoid you. Regardless of how sincere we are, continually putting pressure on people to change, believe or get saved can turn them away.

I'm good at arguing my case. I can passionately defend what I believe. But we must be spiritually sensitive and know when to talk and when to be quiet! We are not called to argue about the gospel but to live it and preach it.

Never forget: One of the most convincing sermons of all, is a life changed by the love of God.

Power to be Witnesses

Jesus said that we would be witnesses when the Holy Spirit comes upon us.

ACTS 1:8 *But you shall receive power when the Holy Spirit has come upon you; and you shall be witnesses to Me in Jerusalem, and in all Judea and Samaria, and to the end of the earth.*

Note that Jesus said that we would "be" His witnesses. This means more than just passing out tracks and preaching. I believe that we should do those things but "being" a witness is a state of "being". It has to do with our identity. When we receive the Holy Spirit, we become something that we weren't before. A witness is a witness when they are working, playing, eating or even sleeping. It is who they are. We are called "to be" witnesses.

After telling my family about Jesus, they could see that my life was changed. I'm sure it's the same with you. But if we keep hammering them over the head and trying to make them get saved, we might find the door closed. Live for Jesus and look for opportunities to share His love. Let them know what He has done for you in a non-confrontational way. People who are not saved can't understand the things of the spirit, but they can see the results.

1 CORINTHIANS 2:14 *But people who aren't Christians can't understand these truths from God's Spirit. It all sounds foolish to them because only those who have the Spirit can understand what the Spirit means.* **NLT**

They can't understand spiritual truths, but they can recognize when something visibly changes. They can see a restored marriage. They can observe and recognize it when someone who was bound by drugs and alcohol is set free. When a foul-mouthed person stops cussing, they take notice. When a violent person turns into a gentle and kind person, it'll get their attention.

Let Them See the Light of Jesus in Your Eyes.

During a court case, a witness tells what they have seen, heard or experienced about a certain matter. You have to know when it's time to testify and when it's not. Witnesses don't testify 24/7. They testify at the right time and at the right place. There is a right time and a right place. If you are testifying when you should be working, cleaning, mowing the lawn, taking out the garbage, doing your homework – or a bunch of other things that I could mention – you will probably experience resistance.

Even though you are telling them the truth, they are not open to hearing it. It was the wrong time. It wasn't time to be a witness with your words. It was time to be a witness with your actions.

Be a good husband, wife, father, mother, grandfather, grandmother, child, grandchild, uncle, aunt, cousin, nephew or niece. Be a good employer, employee, teacher, student and so on. No one's perfect and we are all learning and growing but let them see your progress and growth in Christ.

1 TIMOTHY 4:12-15 *Let no one despise your youth, but be an example to the believers in word, in conduct, in love, in spirit, in faith, in purity. Till I come, give attention to reading, to exhortation, to doctrine. Do not neglect the gift that is in you, which was given* *to you by prophecy with the laying on of the hands of the eldership. Meditate on these things; give yourself entirely to them, that your progress may be evident to all.*

Paul told Timothy to "be an example". He said, "Let everyone see that you are progressing and growing." In other words, practice what you preach. Practicing what we preach, being good examples and letting people see that we are growing and progressing in Christ are principles that apply to all of us.

If you have missed in these areas, that just proves you are still human. (Christians are still humans. They are born again humans but still humans.) If you fall, just get back up, confess your sin, let the blood of Jesus wash and cleanse again. Ask God for more grace to live for Him and to serve Him. Sanctification is a lifelong process. We won't be completely sanctified until we see Jesus face to face, but don't wait until then to get started! ☺ God's grace will help you today!

In a court case, the testimony of certain witnesses can be stricken from the record if it is judged as unreliable. For example, the testimony of a habitual liar can be considered unreliable. A drug addict or alcoholic is almost always considered an unreliable witness. Let's be reliable witnesses for Jesus!

LUKE 12:35 *Be dressed ready for service and keep your lamps burning.* **NIV**

Stay full of the Holy Spirit. Be a living example of the goodness of God. Let them see the joy of the Lord in your life. Let them see the peace of God that passes understanding keeping you calm amid the storms of life. I'm not sure who said it first but:

Your life and testimony

may be the only Bible

that some people ever get to read.

John Wesley, the founder of the Methodist Church, was originally ordained with the Church of England. He crossed the Atlantic Ocean in the 1700's with the goal of converting the native Americans in Georgia to Christianity. Crossing the Atlantic in those days was truly a step of faith. The ships were frail in comparison to the great freighters and passenger ships of today. A great storm arose during the trip, and everyone feared for their lives. Everyone that is, except for several Moravian families on board. They were born again Christians. They calmly sang hymns and songs of worship.

Wesley later recounted the story. *"In the midst of the Psalm wherewith their service began, the sea broke over, split the main sail in pieces, covered the ship and poured in between the decks, as if the great deep had already swallowed us up. A terrible screaming began among the English. The Germans calmly sung on. I asked one of them afterwards; 'Were you not afraid?' He answered, 'I thank God, no.' I asked, 'But were not your women and children afraid?' He replied mildly: 'No, our women and children are not afraid to die.'"* Their confidence and faith in God and in His salvation had a tremendous impact on Wesley.

His time in Georgia was difficult and unfruitful. After nearly two years of work, he was discouraged and set sail once again for England. During this time, he wrote in one of his journals, *"I went to America to convert the Indians; but oh, who shall convert me?"* His own relationship with the Lord was sadly lacking. He was very religious, but he had no peace in his heart. He was unsure of his own salvation. He lacked the confidence and faith that he had witnessed among the Moravian families on the ship.

When he returned to England, he began meeting with a man named Peter Boehler who also was a Moravian Christian. Wesley began to seek God for the kind of faith he had witnessed among the Moravians. As the story goes, in Wesley's own words again, *"On Wednesday, May 24 in the evening, I went very unwillingly to a society in Aldersgate Street, (a Moravian meeting) where one was reading Luther's preface to the Epistle to Romans.*

About a quarter to nine, while he was describing the change which God works in the heart through faith in Christ, I felt my heart strangely warmed. I felt I did trust in Christ, Christ alone, for salvation; and felt an assurance was given me, that He had taken away my sins, even mine, and saved me from the law of sin and death."

That was the moment in which he was born again. This was the start of a ministry that impacted the whole world. The powerful witness of faith that he saw in the lives of those Moravian Christians convinced him that they had something that was real – something that he lacked – something that he wanted.

Never underestimate the power of a life lived for the glory of Jesus Christ.

A Promise for Wives (and Everyone Else)

1 PETER 3:1 *Wives, in the same way be submissive to your husbands so that, if any of them do not believe the word, they may be won over without words by the behavior of their wives, 2 when they see the purity and reverence of your lives.* **NIV**

Peter wrote by inspiration of the Holy Spirit to married women. He gives them some good advice – especially to those whose husbands did not believe the word of God. He tells them how to win their unbelieving husbands. I believe the principle will also work for husbands with unbelieving wives and for every other kind of family member who wants to reach their yet to be saved loved ones.

We can sum up what Peter said with the old adage, "Actions speak louder than words." You've probably heard the old complaint, "What you do speaks so loud that I can't hear what you're saying." This is especially true when it comes to our family members who see us so often and know how we really live. If we are not living what we believe, they'll be the first ones to note it and mention it! Let your life be an example of God's goodness before them and the sermon of your lifestyle will speak more than words can say.

Wives are advised to submit to their husbands – even if their husband does not believe or obey the word of God. I know this sounds horribly old fashioned and unenlightened to our postmodern society and especially to feminist ears. This does not mean that men are better, smarter or more important than their wives. They aren't! It also doesn't mean that wives are to be slaves to their husbands. They aren't. It just means that the wife should honor her husband and do her best to minister to his needs. The male ego can be very needy. Ask me how I know. ☺

Submission in the Bible is always voluntary. In marriage, it simply means to recognize and assume your place in this male and female God ordained relational structure. Both husband and wife have responsibilities toward each other in marriage. We should do our best to fulfill our responsibilities toward our partner in a God honoring way. Regardless of how we view the word submission, there is a promise connected to it for the women who do it.

Peter promises – I'll say it again – He promises – that women who do this will win their husbands for Christ. Listen to the Living Bible translation of this verse:

1 PETER 3:1 *Wives, fit in with your husbands' plans; for then if they refuse to listen when you talk to them about the Lord, **they will be won** by your respectful, pure behavior. Your godly lives will speak to them better than any words.* **TLB**

Peter says the unbelieving husband will be won by his wife's respectful and pure behavior.

Say his out loud: He will be won!

Her godly lifestyle in Jesus will win his heart. He will see the evidence of a life worth living by how good she treats him! A wife who honors and respects her husband is simply irresistible to his male ego.

Polly Wigglesworth, the wife of evangelist Smith Wigglesworth, won her husband back to the Lord by her godly lifestyle. Smith had become so busy with his plumbing business that he had grown cold to the Lord. Polly continued to go to church and live her life "on fire" for the Lord. Smith was deeply convicted by her godly lifestyle. One evening she came home especially late after a church service, and he became angry. He said, "I am the master of this house, and I am not going to have you coming home at so late an hour as this!" She said, "Smith, I know you are my husband, but Christ is my master".

This bothered him so much that he put her out the back door and locked it. He forgot however, that he hadn't locked the front door. She ran around the house and came in the front door laughing. Her joy and laughter were so contagious that he wound up laughing with her. This was the beginning of how she won him back to the Lord. She continued to live for God and joyfully fulfill her responsibilities as wife and mother. Over a period of several months, her faith was put to the test, but she didn't give up. Her unshakeable faith in Christ coupled with her godly lifestyle of love and joy won him back to the Lord.

Dozens of books have been written about Smith Wigglesworth and his amazing miracle ministry, but it could have been different. He could have fallen away from God and died without fulfilling God's purposes for his life. But his wife Polly won him back to the Lord by her powerful witness and joyful, godly lifestyle.

Sowing in Wisdom

MARK 4:14 *The sower sows the word.*

PROVERBS 11:30 *The fruit of the righteous is a tree of life, and he who wins souls is wise.*

Generally said, we shouldn't continually preach to our yet to be saved family members. However, if we continue to live consistently for the Lord and maintain a happy joyful witness for

Jesus, there will be opportunities to sow the word of God into their hearts. Stay full of the Word and walk in wisdom. Be sensitive and watch for opportunities to share the word.

The right word

      at the right time

            is a powerful seed.

      We might only be able to get a word in here and there, so it is important to have our words saturated with God's Word. God's Word will never return to Him void. That means it will produce the desired harvest.

      I have spoken to people for hours at a time and later they'll remind me of a scripture that I shared with them. They heard me talk for hours but the only thing that really stuck with them was God's Word. God's Word has a way of sticking with people. God's Word is the incorruptible seed that will always bring a harvest.

      Wisdom knows to wait for the right season to plant. When the season is right, plant the seed of God's Word into the hearts of your loved ones. Don't continually preach at them. Sow seeds in the season of sowing! The seed may require time to grow but you can be sure of one thing – it will grow. God's word is both the seed and the water that causes the seed to grow.

ISAIAH 55:10-11 *For as the rain comes down, and the snow from heaven, and do not return there, but water the earth, and make it bring forth and bud, that it may give seed to the sower and bread to the eater, So shall My word be that goes forth from My mouth; It shall not return to Me void, but it shall accomplish what I please, and it shall prosper in the thing for which I sent it.*

      If we consistently live the gospel, the time will come when our family members open the door to a conversation about Jesus. Perhaps it will start with them asking a question. In those times, let's make sure we are ready to wisely share the love of Jesus with the rights words. Don't try to kick the doors open. Your joyful, godly lifestyle is the key that will unlock doors that no amount of preaching, pressuring and pushing can.

Petra and Erwin: A Faithful Wife Wins Her Husband for Jesus

Before we close this chapter, let me tell you about Erwin and Petra. Petra grew up in the Roman Catholic Church. She remembers seeing the crucifix but she said that she never really understood why Jesus had to hang on the cross. She learned the Apostle's Creed by heart, but it really didn't mean much to her. She grew up, fell in love with Erwin and they married.

They lived in an apartment in a small town in Austria called Sarleinsbach. Her neighbor happened to be a woman from our church. She invited Petra to a Bible study in her home. Petra learned quickly and became hungry for more of God. She gave her life to Jesus and started coming to church on Wednesday evenings with her neighbor.

Erwin didn't really care at first, but he started to notice that Petra was becoming increasingly interested in "religion" as he called it. Petra didn't talk much about it but eventually she invited him to church. The church service that they attended was very charismatic and extremely unusual for someone whose only experience with the church had been the Roman Catholic Mass. Erwin thought, "These people are crazy!" On the drive home, they didn't say a word to each other, but he determined in his mind that he would never attend church with her again. It was simply too much!

After that experience, they didn't talk about Petra's newly found faith for a long time. Erwin wasn't interested and didn't want to hear about it. He felt like Jesus and the church were taking his wife from him. Petra continued to do her best to fulfill her responsibilities as a wife and mother. She also continued to study the Bible with her neighbor and go to church Wednesday evenings as often as she could.

She came across the scripture in **Proverbs 25:24** where it says, *"It is better to dwell in a corner of a housetop, than in a house shared with a contentious woman."* After reading that scripture she determined that she wouldn't be contentious about her faith or try to pressure Erwin to get saved. Instead, she prayed for him and asked God to open his eyes to Jesus and save him.

Although Erwin didn't understand or even like what Petra was experiencing, he recognized how important it was for her. Shortly before her next birthday, he asked their neighbor, if she knew of something Petra might like for her birthday. He thought that he could get her a "religious book" or something "faith" oriented. She told him that the church they attended offered a correspondence Bible school course and that Petra had mentioned to her more than once that she wanted it. He bought her the Bible course according to the motto, "Happy wife, happy life." For him it was just a religious birthday present for his increasingly religious wife. "It's not for me but if it makes her happy, then so be it." Petra was nonetheless amazed on her birthday and joyfully thanked Erwin and God.

After she completed the correspondence course, she wanted to attend the advanced training program that the school offered. This time, she would have to attend the school in person because there was no correspondence program for the advanced training. Again, to her surprise, Erwin paid her tuition for the school. Later he admitted that he did this in part, because he wanted to attend a course on web design and thought it would be easier to justify it, if he paid for her Bible school course. ☺

Petra continued to grow in faith. As it is with all marriages, they had their occasional disagreements, but Petra had changed. When she noticed that things were escalating, she would stop talking. She often asked for forgiveness, even when she hadn't started the argument. Erwin liked that! Even though he still wasn't interested in Jesus or the Bible, he saw the positive changes that Petra's faith was making in her life.

One day she told him that she wanted to go to church on Sundays too and take the children with her. They talked about it for a while, but Erwin was not excited about the idea. He didn't like it at all! Sunday was their family day. Finally, Petra said, "Erwin, you are the most important person in the world to me, but I can't make it without God." Again, he wasn't thrilled with the idea, but he figured that if she really needed it, he could "put up" with it.

The web design course turned out to be more of a challenge than Erwin had anticipated. He was still working full time and studying on the side. He felt stressed and somehow worried that he might not complete the course successfully. Up until this time he had always excelled and succeeded at everything he put his hand to. But now he was feeling overwhelmed. One day when the pressure was especially heavy, he asked Petra, "How are you able to stay so peaceful and steady?" Without having to think about it, she answered, "The Lord. He gives me the strength and peace that I need." She went further and said, "God can help you too." And He did. Erwin completed the course and received his certificate in web design.

Petra always stored her Bible School books and notes in a drawer. She didn't leave them out because, she didn't want to instigate an unnecessary discussion. She also didn't want Erwin to feel like she was pressuring him. She didn't know it, but from time to time he opened the drawer to see what books she was reading and to glance at her notes.

When she completed the Bible school's advanced training program, she asked Erwin to attend her graduation. She wore a red graduation robe and sat with the other graduates during the ceremony. It was very hot in the building, and she thought that Erwin looked a bit peeved. She had been praying for Erwin for a long time now but outwardly, it didn't seem like anything was really changing.

The ceremony was long with various program points. When Petra went forward to receive her diploma, Erwin applauded her. At the end of the ceremony, the moderator extended an invitation to receive Jesus Christ. He said that if anyone present had never made Jesus Christ the Lord of their lives that they could pray a prayer with him to do so. He asked people to raise their hand if they wanted to give their lives to Jesus. Several people raised their hands and then they prayed.

Petra hadn't been able see if Erwin had raised his hand or prayed when everyone else prayed the prayer of salvation. She hoped in her heart that he did but was afraid to ask him. To her surprise, on the way home Erwin said matter-of-factly, "I prayed that prayer tonight too." Petra was surprised but also overjoyed! From that day on Erwin was a different man. He had been born again. Petra had prayed 6 years for that day!

Sometime later, Erwin also attended Bible school. Together they helped plant a church near their hometown and have built one of the strongest charity works in Austria. They provide hot meals, clothing, groceries, financial and social help of all kinds to people in need. Jesus is in the center of everything they do. They are a strong team for the Lord! It all started when a woman, wife and mother found Jesus and determined to share the gospel with her husband and family through the witness of her changed life. She didn't preach much, and she didn't nag. Her changed life and loving actions preached a sermon that was loud, attractive and effective.

Dear friend, this will work for you too! Never give up!

ANOINTED, APOINTED LABORERS

Matthew 9:35-38 *Then Jesus went about all the cities and villages, teaching in their synagogues, preaching the gospel of the kingdom, and healing every sickness and every disease among the people. But when He saw the multitudes, He was moved with compassion for them, because they were weary and scattered, like sheep having no shepherd. Then He said to His disciples, "The harvest truly is plentiful, but the laborers are few. Therefore, pray the Lord of the harvest to send out laborers into His harvest."*

Jesus was moved with compassion when He saw the multitudes of tired, lost and confused people wandering around and wasting their lives. They had no idea why they were living or what they were living for. Their life was mere existence. They were trying to find purpose and meaning in all the wrong activities and pursuits. If He was moved with compassion back then, how much more is He moved with compassion today!

What did He tell His disciples to do about it? PRAY! Pray to the Lord of the Harvest that He would thrust laborers into the harvest field. God is able to equip, motivate and empower people to go to the lost and dying multitudes.

Although our family members might not be so receptive to our preaching, that doesn't necessarily mean that they won't listen to someone else. Jesus told the disciples to pray that the Lord of the Harvest would send laborers into His harvest. Your family is a part of His harvest field so it is scriptural and right to pray that God would send anointed, appointed laborers to share the gospel with them.

Everyone has a unique personality. Everyone has specific qualities. We all have likes, dislikes, interests and hobbies. Did you know that some people relate to certain people more than they do to others? This is true for all of us. Even as believers, we have our favorite preachers, teachers and singers. For some reason it is easier for us to receive from certain people than it is from others.

We can pray that the Father would send the right laborers across the path of our loved ones. Pray that He'll send someone that that they can relate to. Someone that will know how to reach them and touch their heart with the love of God. Someone that has the wisdom to know what to say and when to say it.

God has people from all walks of life that He can dispatch and lead to your stray family members. There is a laborer that will have the right approach and the right personality to speak into the lives of your relatives.

I was a professional musician playing in the Casinos in New Jersey. God sent one of His laborers to me who "coincidentally" was a musician. He was a great guitarist and "just happened" to be working at the same Casino where we played. It was a real encouragement for me to discover that someone I could relate to and respected as a peer was a Christian.

Until that time, I thought that being a Christian had to be the most boring life on the planet. I was convinced that anything that had to do with fun was against the rules of Christianity. They seemed to have a very long list of things that you weren't allowed to do. Their list of forbidden activities was an accurate description of my daily routine! ☺ I just couldn't relate to most Christians.

When I had my encounter with Jesus at Christmastime in 1983, I really didn't know what to do with it all. I started reading the Bible but I couldn't imagine becoming a Christian or being what I thought a Christian was supposed to be. I was still doing drugs, smoking and drinking when I met Bob Zide. He was playing in a band called "Florida" and they were playing the prime-time hours at the Casino. We played back-to-back many times, so we got to know each other. We would hang around and talk between shows. He always had something interesting to say about life and always mentioned Jesus.

Franny, our bass player, got saved first and his life was totally changed. He immediately stopped taking drugs and sleeping around. The most amazing thing, however, was how happy he was. Instead of snorting coke, drinking, popping pills and smoking joints he was reading the Bible and smiling like everything was cool. He found something that brought him real joy!

Bob started intentionally hanging around to talk to us more often. He saw that God was working in our lives and wanted to help us. He was happy too! He seemed to know what his life was all about. He and his wife Peggy were just cool people. They were living life on the road and travelling with a band just like I was.

They talked to Judy and me about Jesus in terms that we could relate to. Jesus wasn't religious and boring. Jesus loved sinners like us. Their testimony combined with Franny's radical transformation had a major impact on my life. Judy and I were ripe for the harvest the summer of 1984. God used Bob and Franny as laborers in His harvest.

I got saved at Harrah's Casino. Let that sink in for a minute. I didn't get saved at church but at a casino. No matter where your lost family members are right now, God can send someone to them. He has people everywhere. They might run, they might hide but they can't get away from God! My sister and the church she attended were praying for me and God dispatched the right harvest workers to help me find my way to Jesus. I believe He'll do the same thing for your family!

Anointed, Appointed Laborers

Esther 4:14b Who knows whether you have come to the kingdom for such a time as this?"

Queen Esther was an anointed and appointed laborer in God's plan to deliver Israel from their enemies. She was at the right place at the right time with the right message. She had come into the kingdom for that specific time and that specific purpose. Being the queen, she had access to the king's throne room that others did not. She had the right qualifications to fulfill God's purposes.

God has anointed, appointed laborers that He can send to the right place, at the right time, with the right message for your yet to be saved family members. He has someone on His crew with the right qualifications to share the good news with your family. Pray the Lord of the harvest and He'll send laborers to them.

Norvel Hayes spoke of how he came to know Jesus. He was a wealthy businessman and felt like he didn't need God. He said that poor and middle-class people tried to convince him that he needed Jesus, but he never listened to them. He said that it looked like he was doing better without Jesus than they were doing with Jesus.

Of course, we know that financial success has nothing to do with eternal salvation, but he just couldn't relate to the Christians he knew. The god of this world had blinded him, and he was only thinking in terms of temporal success. His thoughts were not on eternity but on money. Most of the Christians he knew were poor and that was one thing he didn't want to be.

In general, unsaved people judge things by outward appearances. If we tell people that God is a good God and our life is a catastrophe, they will most likely have a hard time believing us.

Then one day Norvel met another businessman who was very successful and very wealthy. The man was a multimillionaire and in worldly terms - even more successful than Norvel. As they talked, he asked the man how he got to be so rich. He wanted to know the secret of his financial success. The rich businessman who had so impressed Norvel was also a committed Christian. He shared his testimony and gave Jesus all the glory for his success. When Norvel heard that, he started reading the Bible and seeking God. Soon afterward, he gave his life to Jesus and became a powerful preacher of the gospel.

This was not just a coincidence. This was a divine appointment. God sent the right person at the right time with the right qualifications to share the good news of Jesus to him. Norvel's motives may not have been right at first, but God used the right person to get his attention. Some people need to know that serving God doesn't mean you have to be a pauper. Jesus had rich friends. He still has rich friends today. He can send one of them to your rich Uncle Harvey who only seems interested in material wealth.

Sometimes people just need to know that being a Christian isn't about turning into a boring religious person. When they meet a Christian that they can relate to, it can be a big help to ushering them into the Kingdom of God. Pray the Lord of the harvest to send anointed, appointed laborers to your family members.

"Father, I ask you to send one of Your anointed, appointed laborers across the path of (insert name) . Send someone with the right qualifications, someone they can relate to, one who will speak to them the right words at the right time. I thank You for it in Jesus' name. Amen.

A Little Side Thought

It's also important that we are willing to be that anointed, appointed laborer for the loved ones of others. Jesus didn't just tell His disciples to pray that the Father would send laborers. He also told them to go and preach the good news. Be a laborer in God's harvest field. I believe that if we sow good seed in this area, we will reap a good harvest at the right time. If our family doesn't receive our witness for Christ, that doesn't mean no one else will. I am persuaded that if we have been laboring to reach the lost and dying in God's harvest fields, we can trust Him to send the right harvester to our family.

Say this out loud:

"Here am I Lord, send me."

PUT YOUR ANGELS TO WORK

HEBREWS 1:13-14 *But to which of the angels has He ever said: "Sit at My right hand, Till I make Your enemies Your footstool"? Are they not all ministering spirits sent forth to minister for those who will inherit salvation?*

God's angels are ministering spirits sent to minister **FOR** those who shall be heirs of salvation. They are not just sent to minister *to us* but to minister *for us*. In other words, God has commissioned them to serve and help us. Most people know that angels protect us from all kinds of danger, but they can also help us in other ways. They go before us, clear obstacles, open doors and influence people and situations for our benefit. At times, they may even bring us a message from God. We need to be aware of and take advantage of this important asset that God has given us.

The writer of Hebrews tells us that angels are sent to serve those *"who will inherit salvation"*. That's future tense. In other words, they are serving people right now, who are not yet saved but will be in the future. God knows all things including exactly who will and who won't be saved. Based upon His foreknowledge He has commissioned His angels to help those who are not yet saved but will be saved at some point in the future.

How many times was your life spared before you were born again? I can think of several situations in my life where I could have been killed before I was born again. At the beginning of this book, I told you about the car accident I had before I was saved. I was totally over-the-top drunk and high. I was driving like a maniac. My car was messed up, but I didn't have even a scratch on my body. Other people have died from some of the things that I lived through completely unharmed.

I am fully persuaded that God spared my life because He knew that I would eventually get saved AND because people were praying for me. Prayer can make the difference between life and death. Our God is a prayer answering God. He sends His angels in response to believing prayer. He knows the future. He has plans for us. His plans are good plans and one of those plans is to save our whole family!

Angels are commissioned by God but also by believers who act upon God's word. Prayer activates angels. Speaking God's word activates angels. Acting on God's word activates angels.

Some people are overly, weirdly, angel conscious and others ignore the ministry of angels altogether. In the last years, there have been books written that almost make it seem like you should be talking to angels as much as you talk to the Lord. Some of this overemphasis has led people on the other side to either criticize anyone who teaches about angels or just ignore the subject altogether. Neither of them is right. We shouldn't overemphasize the subject, but we certainly shouldn't ignore it either.

JOHN 1:51 *And He* (Jesus) *said to him, "Most assuredly, I say to you, hereafter you shall see heaven open, and the angels of God ascending and descending upon the Son of Man."*

Jesus told Nathaniel that the ministry of angels would be a part of His ministry as the Son of Man. Angels would ascend and descend upon Him. Jesus is our example in living for and serving God. Angels ascend into heaven with our requests for help and they descend back to earth, with the help we requested. They aid us in enforcing our authority in Christ. What we bind on earth will be bound in heaven! They can also bring healing, protection, divine direction and exert influence.

This was a part of the ministry of Jesus, and it is a part of our lives and ministry in this world. Angels are sent to help us. We are in Christ. We are His body. They ascend and descend upon the Son of Man. The title "Son of Man" has a special reference to the humanity of Jesus and encourages us that we as human beings can and should experience angelic help!

Jesus said that we would do the same works that He did and greater works than He did. **(John 14:12)** How did He do those mighty works when He was here on earth? By the power of the Holy Spirit, by the word of God and with the assistance of angels. If we are to do the same works and greater, we will do them in the same manner that Jesus did.

Don't be hyper-spiritual and seek angelic visitations. The enemy can appear as an angel of light and deceive people. But on the other hand, don't ignore this important resource that God has given you. Stay balanced and stay with the word of God, the Bible.

Angels can be Commissioned by Prayer

MATTHEW 26:53 *Or do you think that I cannot now pray to My Father, and He will provide Me with more than twelve legions of angels?*

Jesus said that He could **pray** and ask the Father to send twelve legions of angels. If Jesus could do this, we can also do this. We are called to do the same works and greater works. We can pray and ask the Father to send angels.

We can ask Him to send them to our unsaved family members to protect them, to set up divine appointments, to guard them from the attacks of the enemy and to influence them for good. They are sent to serve those who **will inherit** salvation. It is indeed biblical and right to pray that the Father would send angels to serve our yet to be saved loved ones. We have already established from the Bible that God wants to save them! In the language of **Hebrews 1:14** this means that they "will inherit salvation" and that makes them candidates for angelic help!

In addition, praying according to the will of God – which is His word – the Bible - will also commission angels. In a sense, they ascend into heaven with our prayer requests and then descend back into the earth with the answers to those prayers. When we pray according to the word of God, angels hear it and are commissioned by it.

Daniel prayed and asked God for further revelation concerning one of the visions he was given. The angel Gabriel *was sent to bring him an answer as soon as he prayed.*

DANIEL 10:12 *Then he said to me, "Do not fear, Daniel, for from the first day that you set your heart to understand, and to humble yourself before your God, your words were heard; and I have come because of your words.*

When we pray, God may respond by sending an angel to do or to bring us the thing we have requested.

Speak the Word

King David wrote Psalm 103 by inspiration of the Holy Spirit. In the beginning of the Psalm, he commands his soul to praise the Lord. He speaks to his soul and admonishes himself to remember the benefits of knowing and serving God. He lists many benefits that we have in God. Among them, is the ministry of angels. David was keenly aware of angelic ministry. He knew that God sends angels to help us but he also knew that we have a role in commissioning them.

PSALM 103:20-21 *Bless the LORD, you His angels, who excel in strength, who do His word, heeding the voice of His word. Bless the LORD, all you His hosts, you ministers of His, who do His* *pleasure.*

David tells us that God's angels excel in strength and that they act according to God's word. He says that they **heed** the voice of God's Word. To heed means to hear something and carry it out quickly. He explains that they heed the **voice** of His Word. The Bible is God's word and when we speak His word, we give it a voice that the angels can hear. They hear it and immediately go forth to bring it to pass. Faith filled words commission the angels of God.

David also tells us that that they do God's pleasure. God takes pleasure in salvation. He has no pleasure in the death of the wicked.

EZEKIEL 33:11a *Say unto them, As I live, saith the Lord GOD, I have no pleasure in the death of the wicked*

He doesn't want people to die and go to hell. This is not what brings Him pleasure. God wants all people to be saved and come to the knowledge of the truth. God takes pleasure in the salvation of humanity. David tells us that the angels of God do God's pleasure. They do what pleases Him! When it's your pleasure to do God's pleasure then the angels will take pleasure in doing your pleasure. To say it simply and in context with our theme, angels will assist you in working for the salvation of your family members.

In the verses that we read, the sweet Psalmist of Israel said, *"Bless the LORD, you His angels."* He said, *"Bless the LORD, all you His hosts".* Think about that for a moment. Here we have a human being commanding God's mighty angels to praise the Lord. Apparently, it's biblically correct to talk to the angels and commission them. David commissioned them to praise the Lord in this instance. However, we also know that angels are sent to help us in other ways.

Let them know where you need their help! They can protect your unsaved loved ones from the attack of the enemy and his schemes against them. They can spare their lives from all kinds of potential life-threatening situations. Knowing about angelic ministry and understanding how to take advantage of it is one of the benefits of our salvation.

Hosea said, *"My people are destroyed for lack of knowledge."* **(Hosea 4:6)** What we don't know CAN hurt us. God sent His angels to serve and help us, but many have not been taking advantage of this help!

James said, *"But he who looks into the perfect law of liberty and continues in it and is not a forgetful hearer but a doer of the work, this one will be blessed in what he does."* **(James 1:25)** God's blessings are not automatic. We need to know what He has said and then act upon it.

We need to know and do God's Word, and this includes His Word concerning angelic ministry. We can't change the past, but we can begin today to act on the Word that we know and be blessed in it.

Supernatural Protection

Angelic ministry can also come into play in dealing with the enemy. We spoke about our authority in the last chapter five. There is a fight going on in the invisible realm of the spirit for the hearts of humanity. The devil is blinding the minds of those who do not believe. Wicked spirits are influencing people to do bad things. They are trying to destroy people and rob of them of opportunities to hear the gospel.

God angels work together with us for the salvation of people. When we command demons to loose our loved ones and let them go, the angels of God drive these enemy forces off.

PSALM 35:4-6 *Let those be put to shame and brought to dishonor who seek after my life; let those be turned back and brought to confusion who plot my hurt. Let them be like chaff before the wind and let the angel of the LORD chase them. Let their way be dark* *and slippery, and let the angel of the LORD pursue them.*

God's angels can chase those dark forces and put them to flight when we pray and when we speak the word of God.

When we exercise authority and command the enemy to loose people, we must remember that those people still have a free will. They can choose to open the door to the enemy again and invite wrong influences into their lives. Of course, they don't recognize what is happening. They are blinded. But God's angels have been sent to minister for them. They will help us as we are trusting God for their salvation!

I believe we can be more effective in the exercise of our authority in Christ if we take advantage of the angelic help God has given us. Break the power of the devil over the lives of people and commission God's angels to help and watch over them. You can pray, speak the Word or you can just verbally commission the angels to protect them from the attacks of the enemy. God's angels will chase them off.

I say it like this, "Angels of God, go to them now. Protect them from the evil spiritual influences that have been binding and blinding them. Be a wall surrounding and protecting them from the evil spirits attempting to destroy them. Be at their right hand and at their left hand. Be in front of them and behind them. Be above them and beneath them. Keep them completely safe In Jesus' name!"

Under a Good Influence

Angels can also influence people for good. What some people refer to as good luck or mere coincidence can at times be attributed to the work of angels setting up "divine appointments". They can influence people to be at the right place at the right time.

Abraham sent his servant to Mesopotamia to find a wife for his son Isaac. Before the servant left, Abraham told him that God would send an angel to help him find the right woman.

GENESIS 24:7 *The LORD God of heaven, who took me from my father's house and from the land of my family, and who spoke to me and swore to me, saying, 'To your descendants I give this land,' He will send His angel before you, and you shall take a wife for my son from there.*

When the servant arrived at the place where Abraham's people lived, he stopped at the well where the young women of the area came to draw water. Then he prayed a short prayer.

GENESIS 24:12-14 *Then he said, "O LORD God of my master Abraham, please give me success this day, and show kindness to my master Abraham. Behold, here I stand by the well of water, and the daughters of the men of the city are coming out to draw water. Now let it be that the young woman to whom I say, 'Please let down your pitcher that I may drink,' and she says, 'Drink, and I will also give your camels a drink' – let her be the one You have appointed for Your servant Isaac. And by this I will know that You have shown kindness to my master."*

Before he finished praying, Isaac's future wife Rebecca came to the well with a pitcher on her shoulder and the rest is history. This is an example of being at the right place at the right time to meet the right person! How did it happen? Just as Abraham said. God sent his angel before his servant and set up this divine appointment. This was no coincidence. This was the work of an angel.

Another story illustrates how angels can help people to be at the right place at the right time to hear the gospel.

ACTS 8:26-29 *Now an angel of the Lord spoke to Philip, saying, "Arise and go toward the south along the road which goes down from Jerusalem to Gaza." This is desert. So he arose and went. And behold, a man of Ethiopia, a eunuch of great authority under Candace the queen of the Ethiopians, who had charge of all her treasury, and had come to Jerusalem to worship, was returning.*

And sitting in his chariot, he was reading Isaiah the prophet. Then the Spirit said to Philip, "Go near and overtake this chariot."

The angel of the Lord spoke to Phillip the evangelist so that he would be at the right place at the right time to explain the gospel to the Ethiopian eunuch. An amazing fact about this story is that the angel spoke to Phillip when he was in the middle of a revival in Samaria. Multitudes were hearing the gospel and receiving Jesus, but God sent him from there to minister to an individual. God is just as interested in the individual as the multitudes. The apostles arrived in Samaria to help with the work and God saw the hungry heart of a man seeking answers.

He sent an angel to set up a divine appointment!

Irenaeus, a Church Father of the second century, wrote about the Ethiopian Eunuch. *"This man (Simeon Bachos the Eunuch) was also sent into the regions of Ethiopia. He preached what he had himself believed; that there was one God as preached by the prophets, that the Son of this God had already made His appearance in human flesh, that He had been led as a sheep to the slaughter; and all the other statements which the prophets made regarding Him."*

God sent His angel to direct Phillip to be at the right place at the right time to lead this man to Christ. Later this man led multitudes to Christ in his homeland of Ethiopia. Never forget that God is working behind the scenes helping us in the great commission.

When we pray and speak God's promises, He can send angels to set up divine appointments for our family members. Angels are at work in the invisible realm of the spirit influencing people to be at the right place at the right time to meet up with the right person with the right message.

They can even influence people to go to church. Your loved one might be driving down the road some Sunday morning and for some reason unknown to them they feel compelled to stop and visit a church service. We have had this happen several times. People were driving by our church and just felt compelled to stop and visit. They didn't have it on their schedule, but God had it on His schedule. The reason that they stopped in for a visit was unknown to them, but we know that angels are working with us for the salvation of people.

Heavenly Messengers

God doesn't send angels to preach the gospel, He sends us. However, angels can help people know where to go to get the gospel. Don't forget the supernatural when believing God for your family. Some people are hungry for spiritual things, but they do not know the difference between the things of God and the things of the devil. The yet to be saved are often open for spiritual things but rarely for religious and "churchy" things. And I honestly don't blame them. A lot of what is done in the name of religion is not at all good. But God loves these precious ones and wants to reach them. Here's an example:

Acts 10:1-5 *There was a certain man in Caesarea called Cornelius, a centurion of what was called the Italian Regiment, a devout man and one who feared God with all his household, who gave alms generously to the people, and prayed to God always. About the ninth hour of the day he saw clearly in a vision an angel of God coming in and saying to him, "Cornelius!" And when he observed him, he was afraid, and said, "What is it, lord?" So he said to him, "Your prayers and your alms have come up for a memorial before God. Now send men to Joppa and send for Simon whose surname is Peter. He is lodging with Simon, a tanner, whose house is by the sea. He will tell you what you must do."*

Cornelius had a vision of an angel that changed his life forever. Because of this vision he sent for a preacher! Can you imagine an unsaved person sending for a preacher? If an angel in all of his glory visited one of your yet to be saved loved ones, it's possible that they might even call you to preach to them. God has a million ways of reaching your family that you've never dreamed of. What God needs most from us to get the job done is our faith!

Your prayers commission angels.

Faith-filled words commission angels.

Angels help us in fulfilling the Great Commission!

One man told the story about how his backslidden daughter got saved. She had been going to the disco, drinking and doing drugs every night. He didn't want her doing that and asked her to stop. He said, "That's not how your mother and I raised you." She just laughed at him and told him to mind his own business. She said, "I am an adult and can make my own decisions now! Mind your own business."

The distraught father didn't know what to do. He prayed for her, and the Lord impressed on his heart that he should stop telling his daughter what to do and what not to do. Instead, he simply pray for her, tell her that he loves her and assure her that if she ever needs him, he will be there for her. So, he did just that. He prayed for her and every time he saw her, he told her that he loved her.

One night while she was at the disco, she had a vision. She said that the ceiling of the disco disappeared and suddenly she saw the face of a gigantic angel. She was so terrified by the glory of that angel that she ran out of the disco and drove home. She came in the house saying, "Daddy, I know that you're right. And I know that you really love me. Please pray for me." She gave her heart to Jesus that night and served the Lord the rest of her life.

You can pray that the Lord will send angels to your family members. Don't limit God. He has done it before, and He can do it again. And yet, regardless of whether an angel appears to our family members or not, we know that they are working behind the scenes to help them find their way to Jesus. Let's take advantage of this great help that God has provided.

Commission God's angels to serve your lost family members. Speak God's Word of protection over them. Ask God to send laborers to them and to set up divine appointments through his angelic hosts. When you pray and speak God's Word over your family, you are commissioning angels to help and protect to them! Release your faith in this area and God's invisible helpers will help you too!

Say this out loud:

"Angels of God, go forth now and protect my lost loved ones. Influence them for the gospel. Set up divine appointments and help them find their way to Jesus."

ONLY GOD CAN OPEN HEARTS

ACTS 16:14 *Now a certain woman named Lydia heard us. She was a seller of purple from the city of Thyatira, who worshiped God. The Lord **opened her heart** to heed the things spoken by Paul.*

When we have an opportunity to share the Gospel, we should do so persuasively! We want to persuade people of their need for Jesus. We want to persuade them that there is a heaven to gain and a hell to shun! There's nothing wrong with a little persuasion.

Some think it's enough to put the information on the table and let people decide. I disagree. When we share truth, we share to persuade. More than once in the Book of Acts we read that Paul persuaded people concerning the gospel of Jesus.

ACTS 13:43 *Now when the congregation was broken up, many of the Jews and religious proselytes followed Paul and Barnabas: who, speaking to them, **persuaded them** to continue in the grace of God.*

ACTS 18:4 *And he reasoned in the synagogue every sabbath and **persuaded the Jews and the Greeks.***

ACTS 19:8 *And he went into the synagogue and spoke boldly for three months, reasoning and **persuading** concerning the things of the kingdom of God.*

ACTS 28:23 *So when they had appointed him a day, many came to him at his lodging, to whom he explained and solemnly testified of the kingdom of God, **persuading them** concerning Jesus from both the Law of Moses and the Prophets, from morning till evening.*

To persuade others, we must first be persuaded ourselves. Keep studying the Word and learning from the ministry of Jesus and the apostles. See what they did and how they did it. Hear their words and speak them yourself. Augustine wrote, *"What you want to ignite in others must first burn in yourself."*

At the same time, we need to realize that only God can open their hearts. If we don't know this, we might get frustrated and give up. Keep living for Jesus and letting your light shine. God is at work, and it is only He who can open their hearts.

Acts 16:13-15 *And on the Sabbath day we went out of the city to the riverside, where prayer was customarily made; and we sat down and spoke to the women who met there. Now a certain woman named Lydia heard us. She was a seller of purple from the city of Thyatira, who worshiped God. The Lord opened her heart to heed the things spoken by Paul. And when she and her household were baptized, she begged us, saying, "If you have judged me to be faithful to the Lord, come to my house and stay." So she persuaded us.*

God opened Lydia's heart to heed the things Paul was saying. She and her whole house were saved because God opened her heart. Let's pray that God will open the hearts of those who are not yet saved. He has the keys to everyone's heart, and He can reveal to us what those keys are.

He can lead us to speak the words that He will use as a key to open their heart. We can be led to do something that makes the difference, that gets their attention, that softens their heart and makes them receptive.

The Argumentative Atheist

Jim was an argumentative atheist. He was a very intelligent man with a master's degree in computer science. He married late in life and shortly after he was married, his wife was diagnosed with cancer. She died before they celebrated their second anniversary. Jim became bitter and started to drink. Before long, he lost his job, lost his house and landed on the streets, homeless and angry.

I met him at a rescue shelter for the homeless. I volunteered there and led Chapel services, prayer meetings and Bible studies. Whenever I saw Jim, he wanted to argue with me. I have always been gifted at arguing so this suit me well. ☺ He was also a big fan of Beethoven, so we also had that in common!

Even the best debaters get tired of the same old arguments and the stubborn rejection of opponents who are not open to hear. This was the case with me. One day, we were going through the arguments – again – about creation and the existence of God. In the middle or our debate, I said, "Jim, we can talk forever about these things and probably never come to a consensus. But I really like you and I want you to know that I believe there is a God who loves you. Can I pray for you?" He replied,

"Well, even if it doesn't help,

it can't hurt,

so go ahead."

I really don't remember what I prayed but after I said, "Amen" we parted on friendly terms.

I want to emphasize that my prayer was probably not that

impressive. It seemed to me at that moment so insignificant. Afterwards, I felt a bit convicted that my motives had maybe not been that pure. In all honesty, I wanted to end the conversation and kind of used prayer as an excuse to do so. Before you start throwing stones at me, think about some of the things you have said or done to get out of an irritating conversation! ☺

A few months later I was talking with Jim. I noticed a change in his attitude over the weeks and months since I'd prayed but wasn't sure what was going on in his life. He asked if he could talk with me for a few minutes and I agreed. He said, "Fred, things have changed in my life. I am now attending a good church where the people love me. I gave my life to Jesus, and He has been healing me of all the pain that I was carrying around inside of me. The other day, I was trying to determine when all of this started and all I could come up with was the day you prayed for me. After that, things started to get better. I want to thank you."

I am so thankful that God can use things that seem so insignificant to us to open the hearts of people. Even at times when our motives may be other than perfect, God can take our seemingly pitiful efforts and change people's lives. If you don't know that, you've never read the story of Jonah. God doesn't use us because we are perfect but because He loves people.

Jim was diagnosed with lung cancer about two years after this. We prayed for his healing but for some reason that was never revealed to me, Jim wasn't healed. He died and went home to the Lord. I believe in divine healing, and I have seen God heal people with cancer over the years. We are always thankful and full of joy when that happens. When it doesn't, never forget that the most important thing of all is not healing and health. The most important thing is knowing Jesus and being ready for eternity. Jim was ready for eternity, and I know that I will see him again one day.

At his funeral I sang, "The Hymn of Joy" which is based on the famous melody of Beethoven's Ninth Symphony. I know that Jim wasn't there to hear it, but I know that one day we'll be able to sing it together in Heaven.

Ask God to open the hearts of your loved ones. Maybe He'll tell you something to say or something to do that will be the key to their heart. Sometimes it may seem small and insignificant to you, but God can use things that seem small and insignificant to us to unlock their heart.

Healing Opens Hearts

My friend Jim wasn't healed but as I said, I have seen many people healed over the years. Once when Judy and I were discouraged we started talking about all the good things that God has done with us and through us here in Austria. We thought of marriages restored, people saved, lives changed and of many people that God healed through our ministry. Our conversation almost sounded like a chapter from the book of Acts. (A good friend of mine says that we are living in Acts 29. I like that! The book of Acts only has 28 chapters…)

Healing is not the most important thing, but God can use it to open hearts for the gospel. This was Jesus' main method of reaching the lost. The apostles and the early church continued to use this method. Healing is an integral part of the good news of Jesus Christ. We should never be ashamed to offer prayer for the sick. God can use it to open hearts.

A nobleman in Capernaum came to Jesus. His son was sick and was at the point of death. Although he was a high-ranking government official, there was nothing he could do to help his son. He had money, worldly power and access to the best health care of the day, but his son still lay at the point of death. Wealth and worldly power are not bad in and of themselves but there are many things that money can't do.

There are many people today, just like this nobleman from Capernaum. They have wealth and worldly power but they also have a problem that their wealth and worldly power can't fix. They need Jesus' help. Let's read the story carefully.

JOHN 4:46-53 *So Jesus came again to Cana of Galilee where He had made the water wine. And there was a certain nobleman whose son was sick at Capernaum. When he heard that Jesus had come out of Judea into Galilee, he went to Him and implored Him to come down and heal his son, for he was at the point of death. Then Jesus said to him, "Unless you people see signs and wonders, you will by no means believe." The nobleman said to Him, "Sir, come down before my child dies!" Jesus said to him, "Go your way; your son lives." So the man believed the word that Jesus spoke to him, and he went his way. And as he was now going down, his servants met him and told him, saying, "Your son lives!" Then he inquired of them the hour when he got better. And they said to him, "Yesterday at the seventh hour the fever left him." So the father knew that it was at the same hour in which Jesus said to him, "Your son lives." And he himself believed, and his whole household.*

Notice seven important things in this story.

1.   The nobleman heard that Jesus was in the area.
2.   He came and asked Jesus to heal his son.
3.   Jesus said that signs and wonders help people believe. *(Paraphrased)*
4.   Jesus spoke a command of faith.
5.   The nobleman believed the word.
6.   The son began recovering when his father believed.
7.   The whole family believed because of this healing.

One healing brought the whole family to Jesus. People need to hear that Jesus still heals today. He is the same, yesterday, today and forever. **(Hebrews 13:8)** We can ask for healing on behalf of our family just as the nobleman did. Believe that Jesus, who is the same today as He was in the New Testament, will hear and answer your prayers today. The nobleman believed the word of Jesus and not only was his son healed, but his whole family came to believe in Jesus.

When I paraphrased Jesus as saying, "Signs and wonders help people believe", I admit that it was a fairly loose paraphrase.

He actually said, "Unless you people see signs and wonders, you will by no means believe." Some interpret this as a negative statement when in fact it was simply an observation. People who are not yet saved do not understand spiritual things. They are moved by what they can see or feel. This is just the way it is. Signs and wonders can indeed open the hearts of unbelievers.

God doesn't give signs and wonders to everyone. He resists the proud but gives grace to the humble. **(James 5:6)** He doesn't heal people and work miracles as parlor tricks to entertain people. But when desperate people come to Him humbly and in faith, He responds. He can use healing to let them know that He is real and that He cares. Sometimes people who are blinded and who have been lied to all of their lives need something more than a sermon. They also need the demonstration of the Spirit.

We have seen this happen time and again. One day at the end of my sermon, I gave an invitation for those who needed prayer to come forward. Several people came to the front and I began praying for them. One of the people was a policeman who had five herniated disks. He had been in extreme pain for months and it was affecting every area of his life. The pain medication couldn't ease the pain. He couldn't work, his marriage was falling apart, he was in a desperate place. As I prayed for the person next to him, he said that he felt a wind go through his body and the pain disappeared, never to return.

Jesus Christ is the same yesterday, today and forever!

About two months later he came to me at the end of the church service and enthusiastically asked, "Pastor Fred, Pastor Fred! Did you see it?" I said, "Did I see what?" He said, "All the people in the two rows where I was sitting are my family. They're all saved!" His wife, his mother, his sister, his two brothers, their spouses, and several other relatives were with him in church! When he got healed, his wife got saved and their marriage was healed. One of his brothers had been an alcoholic for many years. When he got saved, he also got delivered from alcoholism. Then his wife got saved and their marriage was healed too! One miracle brought a whole family to Jesus!

Here's another story that demonstrates how healing opens people's hearts to the gospel.

ACTS 9:32-35 *Now it came to pass, as Peter went through all parts of the country, that he also came down to the saints who dwelt in Lydda. There he found a certain man named Aeneas, who had been bedridden eight years and was paralyzed. And Peter said to him, "Aeneas, Jesus the Christ heals you. Arise and make your bed." Then he arose immediately. So all who dwelt at Lydda and Sharon saw him and turned to the Lord.*

Aeneas had been bedridden for eight years. The text tells us that Peter "found" him. We don't know how he found him. Perhaps Aeneas' wife came to Peter and told him that her husband was sick. Perhaps it was his father, mother, sister, or brother – we don't know. Most likely however, it was someone in his family. Peter went to him and spoke the command of faith, *"Aeneas, Jesus Christ heals you. Arise and make up your bed."* The man was instantly healed and got out of bed.

The story of this miraculous healing spread like wildfire and *"all who dwelt in Lydda and Sharon"* turned to the Lord. This healing led to the salvation of Aeneas' family and everyone else in two cities! Miracles and healings can open hearts in a big way.

ACTS 28:7-9 *In that region there* (Malta) *was an estate of the leading citizen of the island, whose name was Publius, who received us and entertained us courteously for three days. And it happened that the father of Publius lay sick of a fever and dysentery. Paul went to him and prayed, and he laid his hands on him and healed him. So when this was done, the rest of those on the island who had diseases also came and were healed.*

Publius was the chief magistrate of Malta, and he invited Paul and his team to stay with him a few days. While there, Paul discovered that the father of Publius was sick. Immediately Paul went to the father and prayed for his healing. God cares about your whole family. He even cares about their physical needs!

Paul laid hands on the man, and he was healed. After that, people came from all over to be healed. The healing of one man opened the hearts many others to come to an ambassador of Christ for healing. Healing and miracles are keys that open the hearts of unbelievers to receive Jesus! This will work in your family too.

The Bible doesn't say that Publius asked Paul to heal his father. Paul did it because that's the heart of our Father in Heaven! When Publius saw that his father was healed, he certainly gave his life to Jesus and told everyone on the island about what had happened. Church historians tell us that this healing led to a church being founded on that island.

LUKE 4:38-39 *Now He arose from the synagogue and entered Simon's house. But Simon's wife's mother was sick with a high fever, and they made request of Him concerning her. So He stood over her and rebuked the fever, and it left her. And immediately she arose and served them.*

Jesus healed Peter's mother-in-law. One preacher jokingly said that this is the reason that Peter denied Jesus three times! ☺ No! That's a bad joke! Seriously however, the family simply asked Jesus to heal her, and He did. He went to her, rebuked the fever and she was healed. God loves your mother-in-law! It's biblical and right to ask God to heal our loved ones. He heals because of His great love for people. But the testimonies of those who are healed have the power to turn people to the Lord.

Once we were conducting an evangelistic outreach in a small town in Austria. We had advertised that prayer would be offered for the sick. After preaching a simple gospel message we invited people who wanted prayer to come forward. Several people responded.

One of them was a tall blond woman. Her head was

leaning to one side and it looked like she was in pain. He husband came with her and stood next to her. I asked her what she needed. She told me that she had been in a car accident three years ago. The vertebrae in her neck had been damaged and although the doctors did everything they could to help her, she still had continual pain.

Thank God for doctors. They can do a lot. But when medical science has done all that it can do and it still isn't enough, there is hope for us in Jesus! I put my hand on her and prayed in the name of Jesus. She looked startled and exclaimed, "It's gone! It's gone! The pain is gone!" I'll never forget the look in her eyes. Her husband, standing next to her, started to cry. He had seen his wife suffering for three years and now she was free! He immediately gave his life to Jesus!

If you need healing, reach out to Jesus now. He is right there where you are to heal you. Your healing can be a mega testimony to your family. It's hard to argue with a miracle. If one of your family members needs healing, do what we read about in the stories above. Go to Jesus, ask Him to heal them, believe His Word and trust Him to make them well. Ask if you can pray for them. You can lay hands on them in Jesus' name and expect them to recover.

This is not only for a few select Christians – this is for all believers.

Mark 16:17-18 *And these signs will follow those who believe: In My name they will cast out demons; they will speak with new tongues; they will take up serpents; and if they drink anything deadly, it will by no means hurt them; they will lay hands on the sick, and they will recover."*

You believe in Jesus, so this applies to you. You can lay your hands on your sick relative in the name of Jesus and ask God to heal them. His Word says that they will recover, and their recovery could be just the key that God uses to open the door to the hearts of your whole family.

UNLESS THE FATHER DRAWS THEM

Predestination, Election and Free Will

John 6:44-45 *No one can come to Me unless the Father who sent Me draws him; and I will raise him up at the last day. It is written in the prophets, 'And they shall all be taught by God.' Therefore everyone who has heard and learned from the Father comes to Me.*

In this chapter, I want to talk about how the Father draws people to Jesus. I might need a few minutes before I get to it because I want to clear a few things up first. If you are not interested in theology, please feel free to skip to page 126.

The wranglings of theologians may be interesting and entertaining to some, but the outcomes can be disastrous if they arrive at the wrong conclusions. Someone once said, "The Bible is so easy to understand that you need a theologian to help you misunderstand it." ☺

Just to be fair, there are all kinds of theologians and there are many who are sincere and balanced. On the other hand, there are some who do not even believe in God, the virgin birth, the resurrection of Jesus or heaven and hell. Personally, I think they chose the wrong profession. Maybe they could have been a good truck driver or something else, but they are bad theologians.

One school of theology teaches that before God created the heavens and the earth, He already decided who would be saved and who would be lost – and that there is nothing that anyone can do about it. He simply chose them at random and now we're stuck!

They speak of predestination and election – both of which are words that we find in the Bible – but their understanding of these words and the conclusions they draw from them are one-sided and misleading. They claim that God in His sovereignty has randomly predestined certain people to be saved. These are the elect. He simply chose a group of lucky people to be saved, and the rest are doomed. Although they have invented interesting theological gymnastics to try to get around it, the logical conclusion of their theology is that if He predestined some to be saved, He predestined others to go to hell. There's no way around it. Simply overlooking them, "not choosing" them, "not electing them" would be predestinating them to eternal lostness.

If this is the case, then there is nothing we can do about our destiny or the destiny of anyone else. We would be little more than puppets on a string playing out a script that we did not write and cannot change. If God already predetermined your future, then you are stuck. If He has already decided the fate of our loved ones, we can do nothing to change it.

But this is not the case. No, not at all.

There are scriptures that seem to support their viewpoint. Then again, anyone can find a few scriptures to prove nearly any point they are trying to make. However, they overlook, ignore or "explain away" others that disagree with it. John Calvin is credited with this theological viewpoint although his teachings are perhaps less extreme than others who claim to represent "Calvinism" today. (Just to be clear, Calvin had many good things to say about other subjects and I agree with much of what he wrote.)

Anyway, there are five major pillars in this theological

construct. Sometimes the word TULIP is used as an acronym for these points.

T =   Total depravity
U =   Unmerited election
L =   Limited Atonement
I =   Irresistible Grace
P =   Perseverance of the Saints

There are libraries filled with dusty volumes written about this subject matter, so I will spare you the details and sum the subject up as briefly as possible.

Total Depravity: This point claims that the nature of humanity is "totally depraved" because of sin and therefore no one can truly want God, seek God or choose God. The "T" of the tulip says that no one, by an act of free will, can even choose to seek God.

Unmerited Election: The "U" claims that since are all totally depraved, undeserving and incapable of seeking God, God sovereignly chose to save some of them. God wanted to show His mercy but sovereignly chose to limit it to the "elect". He chose the elect randomly without respect to merit or lack thereof.

Limited Atonement: The "L" claims that Jesus did not die for all of humanity. He died only for the elect of "the lucky ones" as I call them. ☺ They reason that some people will surely go to hell and if Jesus already paid for their sins, going to hell for them would be in essence double jeopardy. (Theology can get so complicated. The Gospel however, is simple.)

Irresistible Grace: The "I" teaches that God's offer of grace is irresistible to the fortunate elected few. Regardless of what they do, how they live, what they believe or how they resist God, grace will eventually get through to them. They can't do a thing about – like it or not – they are going to be saved.

Perseverance of the saints: Topping it off, the "P" claims that those who are saved will be eternally kept regardless of how they live or what they do. Some people have coined this teaching, "Once saved, always saved." In opposition to this teaching, one preacher jokingly said," I believe that once a person's saved, they're always saved, as long as they stay saved."

The reason that I disagree with "TULIP" oriented predestination is because I believe the Bible disagrees with it. Don't misunderstand me. There are scriptures that speak of predestination and election, but you can't separate them from the rest of the Bible – which is what you would have to do to come to the conclusions above.

Yes, people are spiritually dead because of sin but that does not mean they are totally depraved. There are some people who have done amazing, heroic, sacrificial things for the benefit of others.

TULIP theology, however, would say that even though they did good things, the motivation of the heart was depraved – they did it for wrong motives. The claim is that unregenerate people act exclusively for their own selfish ego and pride. Even if they do something good it is only to benefit themselves.

Not only is that a cynical way of judging people, it is also unbiblical. *(Unregenerate means "not born again")* All of the faith heroes in the Old Testament were, by definition, unregenerate, and they did great things because of their faith in God.

They did good things in obedience to God

They did good things because they believed God

They did good things because they loved God

They did good things to please God.

None of that is "totally depraved".

Hebrews chapter 11 is filled with people who did all kinds of good and amazing things. They made choices based upon their faith in God and are listed as role models for us. They weren't perfect but neither were they totally depraved. Let's just look at one story before we go further.

HEBREWS 11:17 *By faith Abraham, when he was tested, offered up Isaac, and he who had received the promises offered up his only begotten son, of whom it was said, "In Isaac your seed shall be called," concluding that God was able to raise him up, even from the dead, from which he also received him in a figurative sense.*

Abraham certainly didn't do this for selfish reasons! He did it because God told him to do it and because he trusted God. He believed God's Word and that gave him the courage to obey.

Maybe he didn't understand why God asked him to offer up Isaac, but he knew that God was trustworthy and would keep His promise. Because Abraham obeyed God, the way was made for God to sacrifice His only begotten Son for all humanity. Because a man was willing to sacrifice his only son for God, God could legally sacrifice His only begotten Son to save all humanity.

Genesis 15:6 And Abraham believed in the LORD, and He accounted it to him for righteousness.

God saw Abraham's faith.

God judged Abraham as righteous

not as totally depraved.

NEHEMIA 9:7-8a You are the Lord God, Who chose Abram, and brought him out of Ur of the Chaldeans, and gave him the name Abraham; You found his heart faithful before You, and made a covenant with him.

God judged Abraham's heart as faithful before Him, not as totally depraved! To be clear, Abraham was not born again. He was not a new creation. He did not have a new heart and had not been made righteous like we have been. He still had the nature of sin in his spirit, but he was not "totally depraved!"

And yes, I know that Paul wrote, "there is none righteous, no not one." But when he wrote it, he was quoting **Psalm 14** and **Isaiah 59**.

ROMANS 3:9-12 There is no one righteous, not even one. There is no one who understands, no one who seeks God. All have turned away, they have together become worthless; there is no one who does good, not even one."

Psalm 14 speaks specifically of atheists and people who reject God altogether. **Isaiah 59** speaks of people who are completely unrepentant. The statements made about them are true but we cannot separate these scriptures from the rest of the Bible.

We read in **Nehemiah 9:8** that God "found Abraham's heart faithful before Him". In **Numbers 12:7** God said, "Moses is faithful in all of My house." Job is described as "blameless and upright" in **Job 1:1**. In **Acts 13:22** God refers to David as a "man after My own heart".

I could list others about whom God said similar things, but the point is this: Abraham, Moses, Job and David were not born again but they weren't "totally depraved" either. They were sinners by their inward nature and yes, they sinned. But they also prayed, worshipped and sought God. They did great things in obedience to the Lord. They needed forgiveness and the new birth but there were also good attributes in their lives. So it is with the majority of the people you will meet.

When Adam and Eve sinned, they died spiritually. Man consists of spirit, soul and body. **(1Thessalonians 5:23)** The spirit of those who outside of Christ is dead and under the power of sin. The soul of man has been affected by sin, but it is not "totally depraved". There are beautiful emotions, desires and hopes in the soul of every human being. The love of family, the desire for righteousness and justice, the hopes of freedom and a good future can be found in the unsaved as well as the saved.

In His "Sermon on the Mount", Jesus spoke to these dreams, desires and hopes. All the people that He spoke to on that day were unregenerate or spiritually dead. They were all sinners. He never said that any of these promises only applied to a few lucky predestined folks.

Matthew 5:3-9 *Blessed are the poor in spirit, for theirs is the kingdom of heaven. Blessed are those who mourn, for they shall be comforted. Blessed are the meek, for they shall inherit the earth. Blessed are those who hunger and thirst for righteousness, for they shall be filled. Blessed are the merciful, for they shall obtain mercy. Blessed are the pure in heart, for they shall see God. Blessed are the peacemakers, for they shall be called sons of God.*

- **Blessed are (all) the poor in spirit**

The poor in spirit are those who recognize their need for God's help. They realize that they are inwardly lacking and need help. They are sinners who know that if God doesn't do something, they are lost. Many lost people recognize that they are lost and are truly seeking forgiveness, love and help. There is a cry in their heart, crying out for the love of the Father.

- **Blessed are (all) those who mourn**

Many people are mourning because of injustice or loss. God wants to comfort them. He is moved with compassion for all who are suffering, not just for the elect. He has no favorites!

- **Blessed are (all) the meek**

There must have been some meek and humble people there that day when Jesus preached this sermon. Meekness and humility are not qualities of the "totally depraved". Jesus didn't question their motives. He didn't say that their humility was just a ploy used as means to their selfish ends!

- **Blessed are (all) those who hunger and thirst for righteousness**

There are multitudes, who are hungry and thirsty for justice in this corrupt and unjust world. God wants to bring them into His Kingdom of peace and righteousness. They are seekers who know that there must be more than this messed up life in this messed up world. They hunger for righteousness. How can that be depraved? Something inside of them has convinced them that there is a better way.

- **Blessed are (all) the merciful**

There have been merciful people in every nation, every culture and every century of human history. Jesus told the story of the "Good Samaritan" not the "totally depraved Samaritan". He made it clear that the Samaritan did not help his neighbor because of what he would get out of it. He was simply a good neighbor!

- **Blessed are (all) the pure in heart**

Who are the pure in heart if all people are totally depraved? If everyone is totally depraved, this saying would be meaningless.

- **Blessed are (all) the peacemakers**

Apparently, there were peacemakers in the crowd. In our day, there are people who hate war, oppression and violence. Some of them don't know Jesus but they are moved with compassion for the victims of war and hatred. They want it to end – and so does the Lord.

I added an "(all)" in these beatitudes because the "(all)" is self-evident. Jesus did not qualify these statements based upon election or predestination. He did not say, "Blessed are the predestined peacemakers" for example.

Yes, people without Jesus are "dead" spiritually, but that doesn't mean that everything about them is depraved. If they are "totally depraved" and incapable of seeking God, then every scripture in which God calls upon people to seek Him are nothing more than meaningless rabble.

And that's just the "T".

It's the same with the "ULIP". For example, the "Unmerited Election" argument would logically mean that God also randomly chose who would spend eternity in hell. That is just offensive and untrue. Jesus said that Hell was created for the devil and his angels – not for people. If people go there, it is not because God predestined them to go there but because they have refused His offer of salvation. C.S. Lewis said, "The doors of hell are locked from the inside". In other words, people that go there, chose to go there.

If "TULIP" theology is true, then the most famous scripture in the Bible is a sham.

JOHN 3:16 *For God so loved the world that He gave His only begotten Son, that whoever believes in Him should not perish but have everlasting life.*

For this to be true, everyone in the whole wide world would have to be able to take advantage of God's offer of salvation. Everyone can be a "whosoever". If everyone can't be saved, then Jesus should have said, "For God so loved the lucky predestined ones, that He gave His only begotten Son."

John 3:16 also destroys the "L" in Tulip. If Jesus' sacrifice on the cross only provided atonement for the elect, then God did not give His Son for the world but only for the chosen few. For **John 3:16** to be true – in any plain reading of the text – Jesus' sacrifice must be sufficient for the whole world – for all people and for all times. If not, then God doesn't love the whole world, He only loves the elect.

Thank God, Jesus' sacrifice was and is enough to save anyone who calls on His name! God really did and does so love the world that He gave His Son for ALL so that ALL who believe can be saved!

We could go through all the five pillars of "TULIIP" and analyze them in depth, but I've already started boring you and that's not what I want to do! ☺ This book is about God's promise to save your whole family and how to take advantage of that promise. Sadly, the subjects of predestination, election and free will have robbed some people of their faith in God's promises.

(Give me just a couple more paragraphs to finish this and we'll get back to the main point.)

There are partial truths to the TULIP statements, but they are only partial. Within Calvinism there are various schools of thought, and some are more extreme than others. What many fail to recognize is that Calvin was a child of his times. In other words, some of his theology was influenced by the events and thoughts of the times in which he lived. He was a Protestant Reformer and the Reformers disagreed with the Catholics. It might be an oversimplification, but the argument can be summed up like this:

At that time, the Roman Catholic Church claimed that salvation could only be obtained by being Roman Catholic, adhering to all the Roman Catholic teachings, partaking of the sacraments from a Roman Catholic priest, doing various good works, confessing your sins to a Roman Catholic priest, doing works of penance to pay off your debt to God, buying indulgences and paying for masses and prayers to be said for you and your family. If you did all of this really, really, good, then – you would only have to spend a comparatively short time in purgatory to burn off the rest of your impurities that you hadn't worked off in your lifetime.

In other words, salvation appeared to be based more upon

your works than on the redemptive work of Jesus. (At the time of the Reformation in the 16th century, there was a lot of corruption in the Roman Catholic Church. (They freely admitted this themselves and later initiated reforms in various areas.)

The reformers discovered and taught that salvation is a gift to be received by grace through faith. In other words, our salvation is not based upon our works but on the redemptive work of Jesus Christ.

This is true – but many of the reformers in their zeal to free people from the errors of the Roman Catholic Church at that time were very one sided. Instead of simply letting the Bible speak for itself, they tried to force the Bible into their preconceived theological construct. They twisted and turned any scripture that referred to seeking God or doing good works into something that agreed with their one-sided view. Their theology was at least in part, reactionary.

What is reactionary theology? I'll simplify it further.

(Before I start, please, don't get mad at me. When I write, "The Roman Catholic Church" I don't mean all Roman Catholics. When I write, "Calvinists" I don't mean all Calvinists Both terms are used as generic oversimplifications to make the point easier to understand. The claims below are also exaggerated to help illustrate what I mean by "reactionary theology".)

The Catholic Church taught that salvation is all up to you.

The Calvinists taught that salvation is all up to God.

You say it's all up to us.

We say it's all up to God.

You say this – we say that.

That's reactionary theology!

Loosely speaking, the Catholic Church taught, "Sure, Jesus died for you, but you have to work real, real hard to be saved and hopefully after a few thousand years in purgatory you'll be good enough to go to heaven – or not."

Again, speaking loosely, the Calvinists taught, "Jesus died for the elect and if you happen to be one of the lucky ones you don't have to do anything at all to get saved. God does it all and eventually He'll get to you somehow!"

That's reactionary theology. Perhaps it's oversimplified and exaggerated – perhaps it's more of a caricature than a characterization – but that's what I mean with reactionary theology.

Neither one of these views is a complete representation of what either side teaches but you would need volumes of boring, dusty books to define it further and that's not my point here. Complicated theology clouds and confuses the simplicity in Christ. It may serve to entertain theologians, but it is not reaching the world for Christ.

God provided salvation by grace through faith. He extends His offer to all of humanity, but humanity must respond. Every person is responsible for either receiving or rejecting God's offer.

We can choose.

We have a free will.

God is completely just.

Everyone has a chance.

But He will not override our free will.

The reason that I went through all of that is that the scripture at the beginning of this chapter **(John 6:44-45)** has been used to destroy the faith of many. Instead of people being encouraged to actively believe God for the salvation of their family members, some have felt resigned to accept that God has predestined some to be saved and others to be lost. They think that there's nothing they can do because God has already predetermined everything, and we can't change that!

They imply that the words of Jesus, "No one can come to Me, unless the Father who sent Me draws him" mean that God only draws the predestined elect and the rest are doomed. Nonsense! (By the way, scripture should be used to build faith in the hearts of people not destroy it.)

How God Draws People to Jesus

Let's read the verse again:

JOHN 6:44 *No one can come to Me unless the Father who sent Me draws him; and I will raise him up at the last day.*

If this was the only scripture in the whole Bible, you might get the impression that there's nothing you can do to influence the salvation of people. If the Father doesn't draw them, then they can't come to Jesus. But how does He draw them? And who does He draw? It is absolutely true that no one can come to Jesus unless the Father draws them, but does that mean there is nothing we can do to help them find Jesus and get saved?

If there's nothing we can do, then why should we go into "all the world" and preach the gospel to "every creature"? **(Mark 16:15-17)** If there's nothing we can do, then why did Paul say, "My heart's desire and prayer for Israel is that they may be saved"? **(Romans 10:1)** Why pray for them if it's all up to the Father?

Yes, the Father must draw them but how does He do that and who is He drawing? Is He only drawing the elect, the predestined, the lucky ones?

Of course not! If we read the next verse, we find the answer to these questions! (It's really not that complicated, folks.)

JOHN 6:45 *It is written in the prophets, 'And they shall all be taught by God.' Therefore, everyone who has heard and learned from the Father comes to Me.*

Note the words "all" and "everyone". They shall all be taught by God and everyone who has heard and learned from the Father comes to Jesus. If "all are taught by God", then "all" would belong to the "everyone who has heard and learned from the Father". Jesus was not telling people that they couldn't come to Him. He was telling them that they could.

Jesus spoke about people being drawn to Him more than once. Let's let Jesus clear this up for us.

JOHN 12:32 *And I, if I am lifted up from the earth, will draw all peoples to Myself.*

Jesus prophesied about His crucifixion in this verse. When He was nailed to the cross, He was "lifted up" between heaven and earth. He took the Hand of God and the hand of man and brought them together.

He said, "If I be lifted up, I will draw all peoples to Myself". He was lifted up and He is drawing everyone right now. If He's drawing them then the Father is drawing them too because Jesus and the Father are One. Jesus exclusively does the will of the Father and therefore if He's drawing them, the Father is drawing them. And who is He drawing? "All peoples".

How does He do this?

Preaching Good News

We already mentioned that Jesus commanded us to go into "all the world" and preach the good news to "all people". This is one way that God draws people to Him. They hear the good news and faith comes by hearing. **(Romans 10:17)** As we preach, God is drawing them. We are God's coworkers. **(1 Corinthians 3:9)** We do our part and He does His part.

Prayer and Intercession

Earlier I mentioned Paul's prayer for Israel. God uses prayer to draw people to Jesus. Paul prayed that his people would be saved. (If God already predetermined who would and wouldn't be saved, it would have been a waste of time to pray for them.) Paul's prayer was combined with a deeply felt heart-desire.

ROMANS 10:1 *Brethren, my heart's desire and prayer to God for Israel is that they may be saved.*

He described his deeply felt, heart's desire in Romans chapter nine.

Romans 9:1-3 *I tell the truth in Christ, I am not lying, my conscience also bearing me witness in the Holy Spirit, that I have great sorrow and continual grief in my heart. For I could wish that I myself were accursed from Christ for my brethren, my countrymen according to the flesh,*

Paul had such an intense love and ardent desire for his people to be saved that it filled his heart with deep sorrow and grief. Their lostness overwhelmed him. He didn't want them to die in their sins and be separated from God. It was a burden that drove him to his knees in heartfelt intercession. He would rather be lost than for them to be lost. This is the heart of a real intercessor. God uses prayers like this to draw people to Jesus!

Prayers like this get God's attention. It is a genuine expression of God's own heart. When Jesus died on the cross, it was God saying, "I will take your place. I will take your punishment. I will die in your place so that you can live." Paul's selfless, sacrificially motivated intercession touched the heart of God.

JAMES 5:16 *Confess your trespasses to one another, and pray for one another, that you may be healed. The effective, fervent prayer of a righteous man avails much.*

Earnest, fervent, heartfelt prayers touch the heart of God. And when we pray like this for our family members, God is drawing them. He uses our prayers to draw them to Jesus. We do our part and God does His part.

In a very true sense, we can say that God is drawing all people to Jesus right now. Jesus has been lifted up, the gospel is being preached, intercessors are passionately praying, and God is drawing all people to Jesus.

One last scripture about this.

ROMANS 8:29 *For whom He foreknew, He also predestined to be conformed to the image of His Son, that He might be the firstborn among many brethren.*

Notice that before Paul mentions predestination, he speaks of God's foreknowledge. God is omniscient. He's all-knowing. Because He knows everything, He knows who will and won't be saved. He knows who will respond to His offer of salvation by grace through faith and He knows those who will reject His love and mercy.

And yet in time and space, He is drawing all people, reaching out to all of humanity, He is calling to them to come and drink of the waters of eternal life. He "so loves the world" that He has done everything necessary to save every human being who has ever lived. But He will not decide for them. He will not force them. He will not override their free will. He respects their dignity and right to choose.

1 PETER 1:2 elect according to the foreknowledge of God the Father, in sanctification of the Spirit, for obedience and sprinkling of the blood of Jesus Christ:

The elect are the elect because of God's foreknowledge. Before He pushed the start button of creation, He already knew everyone who would call upon the name of Jesus. He knew they would be saved. That's where predestination starts.

God never predestined anyone to go to hell.

Whoever calls upon the Name of the Lord will be saved.

ROMANS 10:13 *For "whoever calls on the name of the LORD shall be saved."*

WHOEVER REALLY MEANS WHOEVER!

Our efforts are not meaningless. We are not marionettes. God saw the end before He began the beginning, but He didn't make our decisions for us. He is eternal. He sees and knows all things but He doesn't only live in eternity. He is living in the here and now with us every minute of every day. We are His coworkers. He is working together with us.

God is responding to your prayers, faith and witness right now. He is working through you to draw your family to Jesus! Keep believing and shining for Jesus. Keep reaching out and confessing His promise.

Say it out loud:

"I believe in Jesus; therefore,

my whole family shall be saved!"

TRUST THE HOLY SPIRIT

We are not alone when we are praying for and witnessing to our loved ones. The mighty Holy Spirit is our helper. He has a very important role to play in the salvation of our families. He convicts them and reveals Jesus to them.

The only way that anyone can know that Jesus is alive is by the power of the Holy Spirit. **(1 Corinthians 12:3)** They can read the Holy Spirit inspired words of the Bible and the Author Himself reveals Jesus to them. When they hear a sermon or someone telling their story about how they came to know Jesus, the Holy Spirit can touch their hearts and convince them of the truth.

JOHN 16:7-11 *Nevertheless I tell you the truth. It is to your advantage that I go away; for if I do not go away, the Helper will not come to you; but if I depart, I will send Him to you. And when He has come, He will convict the world of sin, and of righteousness, and of judgment: of sin, because they do not believe in Me; of righteousness, because I go to My Father and you see Me no more; of judgment, because the ruler of this world is judged.*

Thank God for the ministry of the Holy Spirit. He is our Comforter, Strengthener, Counselor, Standby, Helper, Advocate and Intercessor. He is the Greater One living in us. He empowers us to be miracle working witnesses for Jesus. We can do nothing apart from Him. The Holy Spirit does so much for us and has such a multifaceted ministry to the church. But the Holy Spirit also has an important ministry to the world or those who are not yet saved.

Holy Ghost Conviction

In **John 16:9**, Jesus said that the Holy Spirit will convict the world of sin, righteousness and judgement. The Greek word translated as "world" in this scripture is "kosmos". It speaks of the earth and the universe but it also refers to the world system and all those who are a part of the world system. Jesus said that believers are in the world but not of the world. **(John 17:11-16)** We are living in the world, but we are not a part of this world system.

The Holy Spirit convicts the "world" of sin, righteousness and judgment. Every person that is not born again is "of the world". This makes them candidates for this specific ministry of the Holy Spirit.

He will convict them of sin. Notice that the word "sin" is singular. He doesn't convict them of all their "sins". He's not convicting them of alcohol abuse, smoking, cussing or immorality. He convicts them of one sin and one sin only. Jesus told us what this sin is. He will convict them of *"of sin, because they do not believe in Me."* The only sin of which the Holy Spirit convicts people in the world is the sin of unbelief – that they do not believe in Jesus.

This is the only sin for which there can be no forgiveness. Everything else that people do can be forgiven and washed away by the blood of Jesus. But if they don't believe in Jesus, they remain in their sins even though He paid the price to set them free. The prison doors are open and the way to freedom has been made, but they remain bound by their unbelief. The ministry of the Holy Spirit to the world is all about revealing Jesus and the way of salvation.

The only way a person can truly believe in their heart that Jesus is Lord and that God raised Him from the dead is by revelation of the Holy Spirit. There is a major difference between having heard about Jesus and being a genuine believer! Faith is of the heart and not of the head. Many people have heard information about Jesus but do not really believe in their hearts that God raised Him from the dead. The Holy Spirit will convict them of this all-important truth.

People all over the world have baptismal certificates attesting that they were sprinkled with water as an infant. Many think that this is enough to get them into Heaven. They look at it as if it were an entrance ticket. The fact is that if they do not have a genuine personal faith in Jesus Christ, they will die in their sins and go to hell – with or without a baptismal certificate. The Holy Spirit convicts people of sin – not that they don't have a baptismal certificate but that they don't believe in Jesus.

1 CORINTHIANS 12:3 *Therefore I make known to you that no one speaking by the Spirit of God calls Jesus accursed, and no one can say that Jesus is Lord except by the Holy Spirit.*

No one can say Jesus is Lord – and really mean it – or really believe it – except by the Holy Spirit. This means more than just repeating words like a parrot. Some people have learned to parrot prayers but don't understand or believe a word of what they are saying. Saying "Jesus is Lord" in the context that Paul is writing about refers to a confession of faith from the heart.

No one can confess that Jesus is Lord, and mean it with all of their heart, without the help of the Holy Spirit. The number one need in the lives of our yet to be saved loved ones is a revelation of Jesus Christ by the Holy Spirit. They need to know in their hearts that He is Lord. They need to really know that He died for them, that He rose again and that He lives forever. This is the only way that they can be saved.

ROMANS 10:9 *if you confess with your mouth the Lord Jesus and believe in your heart that God has raised Him from the dead, you will be saved. For with the heart one believes unto righteousness, and with the mouth confession is made unto salvation.*

The emphasis on the heart shows us that this is more than mere head-knowledge. The Holy Spirit reveals Jesus in such a real way that we are totally persuaded in our hearts. He convicts us that Jesus is alive and that we need Him as our Lord.

Having a baptismal certificate is not enough.

Being a member of a church is not enough.

Giving alms to the poor is not enough.

Doing good works is not enough.

There are all good things but when it comes to salvation, they are no substitute for genuinely believing in Jesus.

Before we talk about how the Holy Spirit convicts the world of righteousness and judgment, let's take another minute and look at a further aspect of the conviction of sin – singular.

The Good News

If the Holy Spirit is not convicting the world of "sins", we probably shouldn't either. Jesus told us to preach the good news not the bad news. Some people are always telling others what they should or shouldn't be doing. But people are not generally moved to repent because someone has made them aware of all the sins they have committed. Most of them already know that they commit all kinds of sins. That doesn't change them. You can tell them all day long that they are sinning and many of them will only mock you. I know because that's what I used to do.

It's not the knowledge of "sins" that leads a person to repentance. It is the knowledge of how good God is that leads us to repentance. Despite all the sins we've committed, God still loves us and wants us. When the Holy Spirit confronted me with the reality of God's love for me – after all the bad things I had done – it touched my heart in a way that nothing else ever had. How could He still love me? His love, mercy, kindness and goodness made me want to give Him my life!

ROMANS 2:4 *Or do you despise the riches of His goodness, forbearance, and longsuffering, not knowing that the goodness of God leads you to repentance?*

I heard about a group of "Christians" that were protesting in front of an abortion clinic. I am totally pro-life and respect the rights of those who want to participate in protests against abortion. I have been to pro-life rallies myself. But the "Christians" I'm referring to, were carrying signs outside an abortion clinic that read, "God hates Dr. Miller the baby killer." That is not the kind of sign that a Christian should carry. God does not hate Dr. Miller. He loves Dr. Miller even though Dr. Miller is doing something that He hates. *(Dr. Miller is not his real name.)*

One of the biggest and most important truths of the gospel is that God has reconciled the world to Himself by the sacrifice of Jesus Christ. Our ministry is the ministry of reconciliation, not the ministry of condemnation. We are here to tell people how to get free from guilt and shame, not to heap even more guilt and shame upon them.

2 CORINTHIANS 5:18-20 *Now all things are of God, who has reconciled us to Himself through Jesus Christ, and has given us the ministry of reconciliation, that is, that **God was in Christ reconciling the world to Himself**, not imputing their trespasses to them, and has committed to us the word of reconciliation. Now then, we are ambassadors for Christ, as though God were pleading through us: we implore you on Christ's behalf, be reconciled to God.*

If God has reconciled the world to Himself, then He's not mad at them and He doesn't hate them. Jesus paid the penalty for all the sins of all people for all times. This is what He meant when He said on the cross, "It is finished". In the Greek, the word for "It is finished" is "tetelestai". It speaks of something being completed. This word was also used in bookkeeping during the times of Jesus. It was written un business documents and receipts to indicate that a bill was paid in full. The penalty that we deserved has been paid in full. There is nothing left to pay.

This is the message we are called to preach. God has reconciled the whole world to Himself. My spiritual father used to say, "There's no sin problem, there is a sinner problem." In other words, the problem of sin has been solved and sinners need to know that God's door is open to them! They can come to Him as they are. He is not holding their sins against them. He is not mad at them. He is calling them home and is ready to welcome them with loving arms. The apostle John said this as well.

1 JOHN 2:1-2 *My little children, these things I write to you, so that you may not sin. And if anyone sins, we have an Advocate with the Father, Jesus Christ the righteous. And He Himself is the propitiation for our sins, and not for ours only but also for the whole world.*

Jesus is the propitiation for our sins and for those of the whole world! The word "propitiation" means an appeasement. In ancient Greek literature, the word literally refers to a sacrifice offered to remove one's guilt and earn the favor of a god.

Humanity did not have to earn God's favor because He has always been favorable to those who sought Him in faith. But humanity was sinful, and sin had to be punished. God is just and, in His justice, He could not overlook sin. All people were guilty before God and deserving of punishment. But God! In His great love, Jesus came to us and offered Himself as the sacrifice for our sins. He removed our guilt and reconciled us to God.

The chorus of the beautiful hymn written by Elvina M. Hall titled, Jesus Paid it All" sums it up.

> Jesus paid it all,
> All to Him I owe;
> Sin had left a crimson stain,
> He washed it white as snow.

The Holy Spirit is not convicting the world of all their sins. The problem of sin was solved when Jesus died on the cross. He only convicts them of one sin because that one sin keeps them from being reconciled to God. God is waiting with open arms but now it is up to each person to believe in Jesus and be reconciled to God.

I preached this message many years ago at John 3:16 Rescue Mission in Tulsa, Oklahoma, where I often volunteered. Among other things, I said, "The wall that separated man from God has been broken down. God has reconciled the world to Himself by Jesus. He's not holding your sins against you! He's not mad at you! You can come to Him as you are." Suddenly, a homeless man in the crowd jumped up and said, "I've never heard that in my whole life!" I was shocked! To think that there was a man in Tulsa, Oklahoma who had never heard the simple good news of Jesus.

Tulsa is sometimes referred to as the "Buckle of the Bible Belt" in the USA. There are approximately 7000 churches in the city, including several mega-churches. Yet there are people in Tulsa who have yet to hear the good news of reconciliation. That being the case in Tulsa, imagine many people there are all over the world who have yet to hear of the goodness, generosity, amazing love and grace of God.

Let the Holy Spirit do the convicting and let us preach the good news! Yes, God hates sin, but He loves the sinner. Our message is not condemnation, it is freedom from condemnation through faith in Jesus. Everyone knows **John 3:16** but **John 3:17** is just as important.

JOHN 3:17 *For God did not send His Son into the world to condemn the world, but that the world through Him might be* *saved.*

Jesus came to save and not to condemn. The only people Jesus condemned were the "religious" people of His day – the Pharisees – those who thought they were better and holier than everyone else.

Before I got saved there were many Christians who preached at me. Many of them preached the bad news instead of the good news. They told me that I was a sinner and that I was on my way to hell. That's not exactly the good news! ☺ I already knew I was a sinner. I was totally sure that I wasn't on the road to heaven! I was even proud of it. So are many other sinners.

> **The good news is that Jesus died in our place so that we don't have to go to hell.**

> **The good news is that God is not angry with the sinner.**

> **The good news is that Jesus paid the price in full for all of our sins.**

> **The good news is that the barrier that separated us from God has been forever destroyed.**

> **The good news is that while we were yet sinners Christ died for us!**

ROMANS 5:8 *But God demonstrates His own love toward us, in that while we were still sinners, Christ died for us.*

God didn't wait for us to get good enough. He loved us while we were still sinners. His love is unconditional, perfect and eternal. No one can be good enough to earn salvation, but no one can be so bad that they are disqualified. Salvation is a free gift to all who call upon the name of the Lord. **(Rom.10:13)** We need to stay good news minded.

I'm not saying that we can't talk about sin or preach

against sin. Of course, we can and should do that. But we are not to be judgmental. It is not our job to convict people of sins. It is our job to tell them the good news that God has reconciled the world to Himself. He is calling all sinners to come as they are and receive forgiveness, love, redemption and eternal life.

Trust Him

We can trust the Holy Spirit to reveal Jesus to our loved ones in response to our prayers and as the Word is shared with them through various sources. It is totally acceptable and good to pray that the Father would send the Holy Spirit to convict our family members of their unbelief in Jesus. The Holy Spirit will reveal Jesus and all that He has done for them.

Righteousness is Right

JOHN 16:8 *And when He has come, He will convict the world of sin, and of righteousness, and of judgment:*

The Holy Spirit will also convict the world of righteousness. In other words, He will witness to them that righteousness is right. He will show them the difference between human self-righteousness and the righteousness of God. Apart from God, our best efforts at righteousness are like filthy rags.

ISAIAH 64:6 *But we are all like an unclean thing, and all our righteousnesses are like filthy rags; we all fade as a leaf, and our iniquities, like the wind, have taken us away.*

Many people have a standard of righteousness that is based on comparing themselves with the worst things that others have done. They think, "I never murdered anyone, never robbed a bank and never sold drugs to children, so I'm pretty good." If you ask them if they believe they'll go to heaven when they die, they say, "I hope so. I'm not perfect but I'm not as bad as others." The Holy Spirit can convict them that their standard of righteousness is insufficient.

Oh, how we need this in the Western world!

In comparison with God's righteousness, our righteousness is like filthy rags. The Holy Spirit will convict the sinner of this. Our works will not be compared to those of other human beings, but they will be compared with God's own righteousness. Anything less than perfection is inadequate. James tells us that if we have broken one of God's commandments, we have broken them all.

JAMES 2:10 *For whoever shall keep the whole law, and yet stumble in one point, he is guilty of all.*

This is the standard – complete perfection. The Holy Spirit does not convict them of righteousness so that they will try to do better – although that's not a bad goal. He convicts them of righteousness so that they will see their need for Jesus.

JOHN 16:10 (The Holy Spirit will convict them) *of righteousness, because I go to My Father and you see Me no more;*

When Jesus was on earth, people saw perfection. They could see with their own eyes what righteousness looked like. Jesus never sinned. He always walked in the perfect will of the Father.

This is one of the reasons that the Pharisees hated him.

They thought that they were

the good ones,

the religious ones,

the holy ones –

that is, until they saw Jesus.

His life and His being convicted them of righteousness. They were able to compare their righteousness with the righteousness that God expects of people, and they were convicted big time.

Now, Jesus is seated in Heaven at the right hand of the Father. We can't see Him right now, but the Holy Spirit has been sent to convict people of righteousness. Pray that He will do this in your family.

At the same time, He will show them the way to obtain the righteousness that comes from God only. Righteousness is having a right standing before God. It is the ability to stand in the presence of God with no sense of guilt, shame or inferiority. The Holy Spirit will reveal that true right standing before God has been made available by faith in Jesus.

2 CORINTHIANS 5:21 For He made Him who knew no sin to be sin for us, that we might become the righteousness of God in Him.

It is possible to stand in the very presence of God and know that you are welcome there because you are righteous in His eyes. The heart of every human being longs for freedom from guilt, weakness and fear. Jesus provided this by being made sin for us. By faith in Him, we partake of and become His very own righteousness. Trust the Holy Spirit to convict the world and your lost family members of this great truth.

Judgement Day is Coming

JOHN 16:8 *And when He has come, He will convict the world of sin, and of righteousness, and of judgment:*

The last thing that Jesus mentioned concerning the Holy Spirit's ministry to the world is that He will convict them of judgment. Some people live as if life has no end and that there will be no consequences to their behavior. The Holy Spirit will convict them that there is a judgment day coming and all men will appear before God to give an account.

JOHN 16:11 (The Holy Spirit will convict them) *of judgment, because the ruler of this world is judged.*

People laugh about sin. They laugh about the devil and hell. I used to say, "When I die, I'd rather go to hell because that's where all my friends will be". Now I know how insane it is to talk like that. People who say things like that have no idea what hell is really like. There are no parties in hell. There is no fun there. There is no surfing on the lake of fire. It is eternal torment.

Billy Joel wrote a song called, "Only the Good Die Young". In the song he says, "I'd rather laugh with the sinners than cry with the saints." It sounds funny to those who are blind and lost but when it's all said and done there is a terrible future waiting for them.

Some people think the statement, "He will convict them of judgment" means that the Holy Spirit convicts people that Jesus was judged in their place. And yes, Jesus was indeed judged in our place. But that is not what Jesus was teaching here at all.

The Holy Spirit will convict the world of judgment because the prince of this world has been judged. Those who are living in sin and following the devil will see that the prince of this world – their hero – has been judged. If he has been judged, there is no hope for those who have chosen to follow him.

We need this today in our world. People have a careless and casual attitude about sin, but sin must be judged. For those who receive Jesus, judgment has already fallen on Him. For those who do not believe, there awaits the terror and horror of eternal damnation and separation from God.

Let's believe God for an old-fashioned move of Holy Spirit convicting power! He will convict your loved ones who are living carelessly in sin that there is a judgement coming. A day is coming when they will stand before God with no excuses. Only the blood of Jesus can satisfy the claims of justice.

Never underestimate the power and the ability of the Holy Spirit. He is omnipotent, omniscient and omnipresent and He wants to see your family saved even more than you do. Thank

Him that He is at work in their lives. Trust Him to do what Jesus said He would do. Believe Him to bring your family into the glorious revelation that Jesus is Lord.

And don't forget – it's not your job to convict them of sin! He can do it better than you. You do your part – preach the good news – and He will do His part – convict them of sin, righteousness and judgment.

Pray this out loud:

Holy Spirit, thank You for ministering to my yet to be saved loved ones. Thank You for revealing Jesus to them and convicting them of sin, righteousness and judgment. I trust You to bring them into the Father God's great family in Jesus' name.

A PUBLIC CONFESSION OF JESUS CHRIST

MATTHEW 10:32-33 *Therefore whoever confesses Me before men, him I will also confess before My Father who is in heaven. But whoever denies Me before men, him I will also deny before My Father who is in heaven.*

Once, after sharing the message of household salvation, a woman came up to me and said that she didn't believe it. Some people just love to argue with the preacher after the sermon, but I could tell that this was not the case with her. She was serious but also sad. I asked her why she didn't believe that God wants to save her whole family and she told me that two of her family members had died recently without receiving Jesus and confessing Him as Lord.

I asked her if she had been with them in their last moments before they died. She said that she hadn't. She hadn't seen them for several months before they died. I then asked her how she knew that they hadn't received Jesus. She said that they never called her to say that they were saved and that as far as she knew they weren't attending church.

I believe that every Christian should faithfully attend church. To mature spiritually and grow in sanctification we need the word of God, prayer and the fellowship of brothers and sisters in the Church that God chooses for us. But attending church isn't what saves people.

I know of people who genuinely were saved but somehow they never got plugged into a church. Any way you look at it, that's not good. The point however, is that attending or not attending church is not positive proof one way or the other that a person is saved.

There are so many things that we don't know. For example, we do not know what happens in the last minutes of a person's life, when their heart stops beating, and they die. Scientists have recently discovered and proven that the consciousness of a person is intact for hours after a person has died. Many people who have had near death experiences claim that after their heart stopped beating and they were pronounced dead, they were still aware of everything that was happening around them. Others talk of going towards a light and meeting people who had died before them. Hundreds of people speak of seeing Jesus and speaking with Him.

One man was fishing with two of his friends when a storm suddenly arose and capsized their boat. His two friends were both good swimmers, but he was not. He said that he remembered going under the water for the third time and that after that he lost his natural consciousness. When he did, Jesus appeared to him and said, "Do you believe in Me, and will you live for Me?"

The next thing that he remembered was regaining consciousness on the beach as one of his friends was administering CPR. He said that as he regained consciousness he was shouting, "I believe in You, Jesus. I believe in You, Jesus!" From that day on, he lived for Jesus.

Ian McCormack is an amazing brother in the Lord. We got to know him many years ago when he came to speak at our church in Wels, Austria. He told us the story of how he came to know Jesus. Although his parents were believers and had been praying for him for years, he was an atheist. One night he was diving for lobster off the island of Mauritius and five Box Jellyfish stung him. This species of Jellyfish contains enough venom to kill 60 people. When he died, he left his body, and an angel came to him and showed him both heaven and hell. Needless to say, upon regaining consciousness he committed his life to serving Jesus. The angel told him that God wouldn't let him die, because his mother was praying for him. God did not want his dear mother to think that he had died without receiving Jesus.

Although we can't base our faith on testimonies like this, we do know that God is merciful and that our families have a special place in His heart. Who knows all that God might do in the last fleeting moments of consciousness to bring a person into the Kingdom? God can do all things and He is the one who promised to save your family.

Don't Limit God!

We don't always know everything that has taken place in the last moments of a person's life. I read a story about a woman who had become estranged from her father. When he died, she thought that he had gone to hell. About two years after his death, she found a little book while going through some of his possessions.

The book was about the new birth and on the last page, it included a prayer to receive Jesus. At the bottom was a place where the person sign their name and record the date on which they had prayed the prayer. Her father had signed his name and recorded the date on which he had prayed to receive Jesus.

She thought he had died and gone to hell, but she didn't know everything. She didn't know that her father had prayed to receive Jesus but there was written evidence to show that he did. We don't know everything. Always remember that God is the final Judge of all, and He knows everything.

He knew everything when He made these exceeding great and precious promises to us. **(2 Peter 1:4, Acts 16:31)** He even knew how wild some of our family members would be and how difficult the task would be to bring them in.

It is not our responsibility to make God's Word work.

It is our responsibility to believe Him.

Faith is the response that says,

"Amen" – "so be it" – to the promise of God.

Don't limit God! Stay in faith. Believe that God will do what He said He would do. Trust Him even when things don't appear to be going the way you wish they would. He is able to save to the uttermost those that come to Him. **(Hebrews 7:25)**

Confessing Jesus Before Men

I know that some are thinking, "Yes, but Jesus said we must confess Him before men." Jesus did say that but the context in which He said it was not about how we receive eternal life. He was commissioning His disciples to preach throughout Israel.

He told them that they would encounter persecution. He said that all people would hate them because of their faith in Him. Then he said that if they refused to confess Him before men, He would not confess them before His Father. **(Matthew 10:18-32)** It was in connection with faith and loyalty in the face of persecution that Jesus made this statement and not in connection with how a person receives eternal life.

He was not talking about how we receive salvation because if confessing Him before publicly is the criteria for salvation it is no longer a gift of grace received by faith. It would be like saying, "If you do this then I'll give you a free gift." No, with Jesus, "free" really does mean "free".

Some came to Christ in prison and died in solitary confinement. They never had an opportunity to confess Jesus publicly. Others cried out to Jesus on a battlefield shortly before they died. I am sure that many have cried out, "Jesus save me" in their last minutes of their life when no one was there except God to hear their confession.

When Jesus said that we must confess Him publicly, He wasn't talking about the confession of faith that saves. He was speaking of the commitment required of those whom He calls to preach the gospel. Even in the midst of persecution, we must continue to hold fast to our faith and confess His name unashamedly.

Of course, I believe that all believers should confess Jesus publicly. We shouldn't be ashamed of the gospel of Jesus Christ. But you don't find it written in the Bible that a public confession of Christ is a requirement for salvation. Paul said that everyone who calls upon the name of the Lord shall be saved. **(Romans 10:13)** He also says that we must confess with our mouth the Lordship of Jesus. **(Romans 10:9)** But he doesn't say that the only time it is effective is when you have an audience of people looking on.

By the way, "altar calls" were one of the "new methods" that Charles Finney began to use in the mid 1800's. I like altar calls and I use this "new method" myself, but you really don't find it in the Bible. We don't read anywhere that Paul gave an altar call and the people came forward and prayed a sinner's prayer.

Believing in the resurrection and confessing the Lordship of Jesus are the only requirements that God established for someone to be saved. God has made it easy. That's why He calls it a gift. **(Romans 6:23)** A person on his death bed may never have the chance to confess Jesus publicly before people but they can call upon the name of the Lord and be saved!

Again, those who receive Jesus should not be ashamed of the gospel but at the same time let's not add requirements for receiving salvation that are not really in the Bible. My friend Franny used to say, "Religion is man's price tag on God's free gift". In some churches they say, "If you come to our altar, prayer our prayer, be baptized with our baptismal formula, then you'll be saved." That's religion and religion never saved anyone!

The thought behind **Romans 10:9** is not a mere verbal confession before people to prove something. The idea is that we confess with our mouth what we genuinely believe in our heart. Many people have made empty confessions of Jesus as Lord but did not have faith in their heart. Some guys went to an altar and prayed the sinner's prayer to impress a pretty Christian girl. Later it became evident that their profession of faith was bogus.

I believe it is possible that others who were not as outspoken had a genuine saving faith that we will realize one day in heaven. Confessing that Jesus Christ is Lord is not just a religious requirement, it is a statement of what we truly believe.

There are different levels of rewards in heaven and there is also a judgment seat of Jesus Christ before which every believer will stand one day. **(1 Corinthians 3:12-15)** Our works will be judged, and Paul said that some people will just barely be saved and that as by fire – but at least they'll be saved. I believe that we'll all be surprised by some of the people that we might meet in heaven.

This does not mean that household salvation is an automatic reality. Our family must genuinely believe in Jesus to be saved. We'll have to pray, believe, exercise our authority and live for Jesus. Faith is required to receive the promises of God. But if we have done what we know the Bible says we should do and are trusting God for the salvation of our family then we can be confident that God will be faithful to His Word. Even when the natural, outward circumstances are different from what we would like to see, God is working on our behalf and on behalf of our family.

Trust God. Take Him at His Word. You can pray in faith and expect to see your whole family with you in Heaven on that great and glorious day.

MY STORY PART 2

The man in the red socks until now

"Freddy, we've been praying five years for you."

Prayer works. The prayers of the man in the red socks and those of my sister and her husband made a difference. They drew me to Jesus, opened my heart, brought conviction, provided protection, determined divine appointments, influenced me, revealed God's love and brought me to the point of decision.

I was born again on July 14, 1984 at about 9:30 pm in room 424 of Harrah's Marina Casino Hotel in Atlantic City, New Jersey. I've been living for the Lord ever since and am amazed at the good things that God has done in and through my life.

Judy and I were living together back then. We weren't married – we had been living a wild life of partying, drugs, alcohol, smoking, cussing – just wild. When I got saved, she was visiting her family in Kentucky at the time. I called her and told her, "Something very cool has happened but I don't want to tell you about it on the phone. When you get back to New Jersey next week I'll tell you."

The next week, I drove to the train station in Philadelphia to pick her up. On the way home, I told her that I became a Christian. She didn't know what to think about that. She always said that she believed in God, and I always said I was an atheist. When I told her I was saved, she didn't really know what to expect. When we got home, it didn't take long for her to recognize that I was a radically different person.

I had already quit doing drugs and smoking. I found out that I was a new creation and not a smoker. It's so easy for a non-smoker to not smoke! I still tell people today, "I don't smoke! I burn – I burn for Jesus!" She saw the pack of broken cigarettes in a clean ashtray that attested to the fact. A big, brand-new Bible lay on the coffee table with some other Christian books. I told her that I had flushed the bag of weed that I had down the toilet. My days of drug abuse were over! Before I was saved, I hardly spoke a sentence without cussing. Now, I refrained from those off-color words and talked about Jesus, the Bible, love, forgiveness, life, joy and peace.

(I didn't tell her at that moment, but I had also received the baptism with the Holy Spirit and had spoken in tongues.)

That night when we went to bed, I explained to her that since becoming a Christian, I liked to pray before going to sleep. I asked her if she minded. She said it was ok. So, I prayed, thanked God for saving me and asked Him to save her too. And then without thinking about it, I prayed in other tongues for a minute or two. At the end I said, "Amen! Goodnight darling. I love you."

Judy said nothing.

I admit that praying in tongues wasn't very wise of me. I really didn't think about it. I was just excited about Jesus and open for everything that He wanted to do. Judy was shocked. She had heard somewhere that speaking in tongues was of the devil. We turned the light back on and I opened the Bible, read her the scriptures about speaking and praying in tongues and explained it as best as I could. This helped her, but she knew that life would be totally different than the way it had been.

Over the next few months, she struggled with my newfound

faith. I went to church, read my Bible, spent time in prayer and still played in the band. Sometimes she would come to church with me, other times not. Our old friends – I mean our really good friends – friends with whom we took LSD – friends from whom I bought cocaine and pot – I mean really, really, good friends – they told Judy that she should leave me. They said, "He's brainwashed. He needs to be deprogrammed. You can't stay with him. He's messed up." Like I said – they were really good friends. ☺

Anyway, that didn't make it easier for Judy. She wasn't sure if she wanted to stay with me. She was torn between loving me and knowing that staying with me meant a completely different kind of lifestyle.

About a month after getting saved, I was baptized at Union Lake, in Millville NJ. I wasn't scheduled to be baptized that evening, but Pastor Kenyon asked me to play guitar at the baptismal service. Judy accompanied me although she still wasn't sure about it all. At the end of the service, the pastor asked, "Is there anyone else who wants to be baptized tonight? If you've been saved but haven't yet followed the Lord in baptism, tonight is your night."

I asked the guy standing next me – it was the man with the red socks - "Should I get baptized? My mom took me to the church when I was a baby and they sprinkled me with water but after that I lived like the devil the next 23 years. What do you think?" Like a good Pentecostal he said, "Brother, you'll have to know that for yourself." So, I put my hand up, put my guitar down, took off my cowboy boots and leather belt and went out in the lake to get baptized. When I got back to shore, Judy was standing there with tears in her eyes. They weren't tears of joy but rather tears of uncertainty.

She decided to go to Kentucky to visit her folks again and to clear her head. I was nervous and thinking she might leave me. So, I spent some extra time in prayer for her. It wouldn't be right for me to get saved without her getting saved too. We were a couple. We belonged together. I asked God to touch her heart and prayed for her salvation.

When she was there, she talked to her mother about what had happened to me, but her mother wasn't able to help her. Then, she went out into a field, sat on a tree stump and talked to God. She said, "God, I always said I believed in you. But Fred always said he was an atheist. Now that I see how you've changed him and saved him, I'm not sure what I really believed. I love him and don't want to leave him just because he's saved but now, I need to know. If you are real, make yourself real to me too."

She returned to New Jersey about a week later and shortly after that she gave her life to Jesus. Now we were both born again. It was the beginning of a new life for us. We still weren't married but I really didn't think anything about it.

...at first.

After a while I started feeling that it wasn't right for us to just live together without being married. In America, Christians called it "living in sin." I knew that this couldn't be good! I called an old musician friend from California who used to tell me about Jesus before I was saved. I always thought he was a cool Christian because he smoked joints with me, played electric guitar and talked about Jesus. ☺

I told him that I had gotten saved. He was happy to hear that. Then I told him that Judy had also gotten saved, but we were still living together and not married. I asked him, "Do you think that we are somehow married in the eyes of God or something?" I really wasn't sure. He said, "Wow man, I don't know either." Not really a helpful answer.

Anyway, I talked to Judy and told her that I thought we should get married. I was getting more and more convicted that sex before marriage wasn't God's will and that we should just go ahead and get married. But she reminded me that our original plan – when we first got together – was to get married after five years on the same day we met. That would have been May 5, 1986. She negotiated, "We could get married next year (1985) on May 5." This was sometime in September of 1984.

We were both growing in the Lord, attending and serving in church and helping out wherever we could. I was still playing in the band and was on the road a lot. In December, we were playing in Johnstown, Pennsylvania. I called Judy and I was really fighting the conviction that I was feeling. I told her, "Either we get married, or we'll have to get separate apartments until we do. I can't handle this conviction anymore."

I admit this was the worst, most unromantic marriage proposal in the history of the world – but Judy said yes and that's what counts. We got married shortly after I got back to New Jersey on December 22, 1984, and we've been happily married ever since.

We have also been serving the Lord together since then. At first, we served in every area of our local church.

Cleaning,

painting,

leading worship,

children's ministry,

youth ministry,

and teaching.

We organized open air concerts, started a home prayer group, passed out tracks on the streets, ministered in nursing homes, prisons and churches. Many people received Jesus and were filled with the Spirit. Several people were healed. Good things were happening.

In 1988 God called us to attend Rhema Bible Training

College in Oklahoma to prepare for full time ministry. I graduated in 1990 and Judy in 1991. We lived in Tulsa nearly 6 years and were involved in all kinds of ministry again. I preached and taught at the homeless shelter, ministered in prisons and nursing homes, did street evangelism, tent meetings, led worship, organized concerts and preached in several churches. Judy served in children's ministry, helped in our home prayer meeting and cared for our two children.

Our time in Tulsa was very blessed and very fruitful. We had grown and learned a lot about how to reach people and help them grow in Jesus. I felt we were ready for the next steps but wasn't sure what the Lord had in store for us. In 1992, I preached over 100 times while still working my day job. In 1993, I preached 120 times. Since I was self-employed, I was able to juggle my schedule and Judy and the kids were able to be with me many times at the various ministry events.

After a while, I was feeling a little bit frustrated. We only moved to Tulsa to train for the ministry. I thought we were ready, and I wanted to move into whatever full time ministry the Lord had for us. I learned several valuable lessons during that time of waiting. First of all, time spent in preparation is never wasted time. Secondly, preparing for the ministry is more than attending Bible School. It also requires growth in character and experience. At the beginning of 1994, I felt like I was ready to explode with all that I had received. I had to go somewhere and let it all out.

We continued to faithfully serve in the areas that God had opened up for us as well as attend every service possible at our local church. One evening in January as the preacher preached, I sensed God saying to me, "Don't forget why you are alive. Don't forget my vision for your life. Get ready to leave. Soon you will be moving from this place." I was so excited! Immediately after the service, I told Judy, "The Lord spoke to me and said we were going to leave Tulsa soon!" She looked at me and asked, "Where?" I said, "I don't know but I know we have to get ready."

The next month, several opportunities presented themselves. Each time however, I sensed no peace in my heart about them. Somehow, I felt like they were smaller than the thing that the Lord was referring to. They just didn't feel right on the inside. And then in March 1994, the telephone rang at 4:00 am. Judy answered the phone and said it was for me. I got out of bed, picked up the phone and groggily said hello. As soon as I heard the voice at the other end of the line, I knew that this was what God was talking about when He said that we would be moving soon.

The voice was that of one of our friends who had started travelling to Romania. He was planning to move there to start a church and Bible School. He didn't want to fly with the Romanian airline back then, so he would fly to Austria and then travel to Romania by car. He was visiting a man in Austria who had started a house group. This man also wanted to start a church and Bible School. He was looking for someone who could help – someone who could lead worship and teach. Our mutual friend thought of me and they called.

In April, I travelled to Austria for the first time and ministered in the home group. The first evening there I led worship and then shared about the baptism with the Holy Spirit. There were about 30 people there and at least half of them received the Holy Spirit and spoke in tongues. One man was healed of a sickness that he'd had for several years.

They had already found a building and were preparing it for church services. During the next days, I was able to help paint the building, order the first sound system and get to know some of the people. I couldn't communicate in German but with hands, feet, facial gestures and the little bit of English that people spoke we connected.

Judy and I moved to Austria two months later on June 24,1994. We came with our two children, Joshua who was seven and Hannah who was two. We brought 8 boxes with clothes and household things and one guitar. We had about 500 US dollars with us and had no idea how all this would turn out, but we were thrilled to be following Jesus.

Like I said, neither of us spoke a word of German, but we were ready to learn. Judy said that the Lord encouraged her by saying, "Languages are easy – even babies learn them." Someone else encouraged me with the words, "Don't worry. Life is too short for anyone to learn German properly". I started leading praise and worship in German the first week we were there. I learned the songs phonetically and then asked the person helping me to explain what we were actually singing. ☺

Those early years were not always easy. In Austria at that time about 85% of the population was Roman Catholic. Most of them were Catholic in name only. In other words, they owned a baptismal certificate but weren't born again. They had been baptized as a baby but had never developed a genuine faith in Jesus Christ. It was more of a tradition and cultural thing than a genuine faith that saved. They considered us to be a cult. At that time, anything that wasn't Roman Catholic was considered a cult. Even the Lutheran and Orthodox churches were viewed with suspicion!

We had church services several times a week. People were getting saved and filled with the Holy Spirit every week. Notable healings were happening, and people started coming from all over Austria and southern Germany. The move of the Holy Spirit was powerful, and we experienced genuine times of revival.

In November of 1994, we founded a Bible School, which would eventually become Rhema Bible Training College Austria. We had 30 students in our first school year and every one of them completed the course. Since then, many have graduated from our two-year ministerial training program. Many more have completed the first-year program. More than 25 churches have been established, evangelistic, missions, and social ministries have been founded and thousands of people have been saved and filled with the Holy Spirit. Today, we look at what God has done, is still doing, and are amazed.

Don't give up on your family. Maybe it looks discouraging right now, but God has great plans for you and your whole house!

Those prayers of my sister, her family and the church worked! As I think about how God answered their prayers, I can see that God used many of the things I mentioned in this little book to bring me into His kingdom.

- **The devil's blinders were removed**

I'm sure that I was as blind spiritually as anyone could be but there was a hunger in my heart for the truth. I never thought it had anything to do with Jesus but later I discovered that He said, "I am the way, the truth and the life, no man comes to the Father but through me." I am convinced that those who are truly seeking truth will eventually find Jesus!

One December night as my wife, a friend and myself were singing Christmas carols, the blinders were removed from the eyes of my spirit. God touched my heart and for the first time in my life I knew that there was something real and true about Jesus. Seven months later I got born again.

- **People lived the life in front of me**

As I said earlier, my sister had been born again for some time before me. She shared about Jesus, but it never really affected me too much except that it occasionally stirred up my rudeness and argumentative nature. There was one thing however that I knew for sure. She really meant business with God. She was very consistent and faithful to God after her decision for Jesus. I knew that even though I couldn't relate to what she was doing, it was something very real and important in her life. Thanks Theresa!

The bass player in the band I was playing with rededicated his life to Jesus about 2 months before I got saved. He would come in to our dressing room beaming with the love of God and filled with the joy of the Lord. He had been even worse than I was concerning drugs, but after he recommitted to Jesus, he really lived the life. By the way, he still does to this day.

He never really preached too much because he knew that I would argue. From time to time, he would make a comment and I would do whatever I could to try to steal his joy. Thank God that in those times he didn't get mad and fight back. He really kept his testimony pure even amid my cynical attacks. I knew that he had found something that was real. He was the only other person in room 424 of Harrah's Casino the night of July 14,1984 when I gave my heart to Jesus. He was also my best man at our wedding. Thanks Franny!

- **Angelic protection**

I know that today I would be pushing up daisies if it hadn't been for the mercy of God sending His angels to protect me. There were so many times that I did stupid things that should have put me in the grave but somehow, I lived to receive the salvation of God. The prayers of those who prayed for me commissioned angels to protect me! Thank You Father, for your angels!

- **Laborers for the harvest**

In the chapter on praying to the Lord of the harvest, I said that God has an anointed, appointed laborer who has the right words and testimony to share the gospel with your loved ones. Many people had witnessed to me before I received Jesus but there was one person God particularly used in the last couple of weeks before I got saved.

As I already told you, he was a guitar player, and I was a guitar player. He wrote songs and I wrote songs. He was in a casino showband, and I was in a casino showband. Don't let your religious tendencies shock you. God has people everywhere –

even in places you would never expect. ☺ I thank God that there was a laborer in a casino showband.

This brother was someone that I could relate to, and he really played a major part in swaying my heart towards making the decision for Jesus. I saw in him that a person doesn't have to be boring and weak to be a Christian. I realized that Jesus was more than going to church and acting religious. Thanks Bob!

God knows the right people to send to your loved ones. Pray the Lord of the harvest that He would send that anointed, appointed laborer. He has the right person with the right message, and He will send them to the right place at the right time in answer to our prayers. Pray in faith and keep expecting the good report. It's coming!

• **Trust the Holy Spirit**

Through all of this I know that the Holy Spirit was working on me. I was always interested in spiritual things although most of the time I was misguided. None of the other spiritual experiences that I searched out really witnessed truth in my heart but when the Holy Spirit witnessed Jesus to me, I knew that there was undeniable truth in the message. Thank You Holy Spirit!

Many people are hungry for spiritual truth, but dead, dry, traditional religion has dulled the claims of the Church to a great degree. New Age and Esoteric materials are bestsellers because of the Church's lack of spiritual power. We need to trust the Holy Spirit to bring conviction and the revelation of Jesus to these hungry people. Jesus alone can satisfy their hungry hearts.

The Holy Spirit will reveal Him to those for whom we pray.

DON'T STOP BELIEVING

I told you some of my story to encourage you. Never give up praying and believing for your yet to be saved family members. It might look like they are the least likely to ever get saved. That's who I was. They might be the black sheep of the family. Again, that was me! But nothing is impossible with God. Your prayers are making a difference and God is working right now to fulfill His promise to you!

HEBREWS 11:1 *Now faith is the substance of things hoped for, the evidence of things not seen.*

Regardless of what you see right now, believe that God is working. Faith is how promises are obtained. Believing God releases the power of His word.

HEBREWS 11:6 *But without faith it is impossible to please Him, for he who comes to God must believe that He is, and that He is a rewarder of those who diligently seek Him.*

There are two things God requires of us when we come to Him. First, we **MUST** believe that He is. This doesn't mean the general sense of believing in His existence. Demons also believe in God, but they are not pleasing Him! **(James 2:19)** God wants us to believe in the revelation of His Person that He has given us in the Bible. He wants us to believe that He is who He said He is.

Smith Wigglesworth said, "I cannot understand God by impressions or feelings; I cannot get to know God by sentiments. If I am going to know God, I am going to know Him by His Word." Never forget this: God is everything that He said He is.

Every time that we come to God in prayer, we **MUST BELIEVE** that He is. We need to remind ourselves that He is the faithful God who made exceeding great and precious promises. All His promises are yes and amen! He is not a liar. If He promised us something He will do it.

NUMBERS 23:19 *God is not a man, that He should lie, nor a son of man, that He should repent. Has He said, and will He not do? Or has He spoken, and will He not make it good?*

He is faithful.

He is trustworthy.

We must believe that He is!

And secondly, every time we come to God in prayer, we **MUST ALSO BELIEVE** that He will reward us! He will answer our prayers. He will bless us, reward us and fulfill His promise to us.

1 John 5:14-15 *Now this is the confidence that we have in Him, that if we ask anything according to His will, He hears us. And if we know that He hears us, whatever we ask, we know that we have the petitions that we have asked of Him.*

We can and should be confident when we pray. God hears us when we ask anything according to His will. His will is His word. If he promised us something, it is His will for us to have it. He promised that our family would be saved! It is His will that they be saved!

John went on to say, *"If we know He hears us, we know we have it."* That reminds me of Jesus. Jesus said that believing prayer is a prayer that receives the answer.

MARK 11:24 *Therefore I say to you, whatever things you ask when you pray, believe that you receive them, and you will have them.*

In the same moment that we ask, we must also believe that we received a positive answer. We must believe that we received what we requested – and then we will have it. This is not hard! You don't have to try to work something up. You don't have to try to prove that you are a faith giant. All that you must do, is believe that God heard your prayer and said yes. He always says yes when we ask for what He promised us.

That doesn't mean that we will see immediate results in the natural.

We believe that we received it

　　　and then sometime afterward

　　　　　we will have it.

It might be a while before we see the results in our world – in this dimension. But if we want to see results, we must first believe that God has done it.

The best way to ensure that your faith is working, is to continually thank God for the answer before you see it with your eyes. Thank Him and praise Him just as fervently as you would if you already had the answer to your prayer in the natural. Faith praises God for the results before it sees any results. Faith thanks God that He did what we asked Him to do before we see any evidence in the natural that He did it.

The daughter of a couple in our church fell away from the Lord in her early teenage years. She got into drugs, was going out with older guys and living a wild party life. Some of the guys she was with abused her and she got further into drugs just to ease the pain. Her parents never gave up on her. They continued to believe God for her salvation.

After many years of drugs and abusive relationships she wanted to end her life. In that moment, God came to her and reminded her of the love that she felt in church as a child. He reminded her of her parents and friends who loved her. Just at that time, God used our daughter as one of His anointed, appointed laborers to encourage her and let her know that God loves her.

She rededicated her life to Jesus and today she is on fire for God. She is a powerful witness and has won many people to Jesus. Her life is restored, and her parents are rejoicing. There were times when it looked like their prayers were not being answered. There were times when it looked like their daughter was gone for good. But they held on to their faith. They keep on believing that God was faithful. They believed that they received the answer to their prayer and thanked God for her salvation when it looked like she would never be saved.

HEBREWS 10:23 *Let us hold fast the confession of our hope without wavering, for He who promised is faithful.*

After we have prayed in faith – believing that we received what we asked for – we need to hold fast to our confession of hope. Thank God and praise Him that He has heard and answered your prayer. Thank Him that your loved one is saved with the same enthusiasm and sincerity as you would if they were already serving Jesus and going to church with you every Sunday!

HEBREWS 10:35-36 *Therefore do not cast away your confidence, which has great reward. For you have need of endurance, so that after you have done the will of God, you may receive the promise:*

NEVER GIVE UP!

Your faith will be rewarded.

God promised.

It cannot be otherwise.

We'll need some endurance along the way. Jesus didn't say, "Believe that you received it and you will IMMEDIATELY have it". Especially when we are praying for people, we need some patience. There are often things that need to happen, divine appointments that must take place, experiences that must transpire, things that they need to hear to bring about the change in their heart. But all the time God is working. Don't stop believing. Hold on to His promise. Hold fast to that which you received! You will have it!

Since Judy and I received Jesus, other family members have also been saved. My mother, two of my brothers, a sister-in-law, my father-in-law, mother-in-law, both of Judy's brothers, three of her aunts, her grandmother and several of her cousins have come into the family of God. We know that the rest of them are on their way. They too shall be saved.

God is a God of families and as a believer, our family is priority to Him. Dare to believe the promise and begin to pray earnestly for your loved ones.

ACTS 16:31 *Believe on the Lord Jesus Christ and you will be saved and your whole house!*

A PRAYER FOR YOUR FAMILY

I am not a big fan of reading prayers that someone else has written but I've included this prayer as an example that you may use. I believe that if you pray this prayer and connect it to the faith in your heart, you'll be on the right track. Of course, the best thing would be for you to get the spirit of this message burning in your heart. Then you can pour out your heart to God in your own words.

Let's Pray

"Father God, I thank You in the name of Jesus that household salvation is a covenant right. You said in Your Word that if I believe on the Lord Jesus Christ, I will be saved as well as my whole household. I trust You now to bring this to pass in my family.

Devil, I command you in the name of Jesus to take your hands off my family. I break your power and influence over their lives and bind you in Jesus' name. Take the blinders off their minds now, in the name of Jesus.

Lord Jesus, I thank You for filling me with the Holy Spirit and making me a good witness to my family members. Help me to live a life that is a testimony to your power, goodness and joy. Let your light shine through me.

Father, You are the Lord of the harvest and I ask you to send anointed, appointed laborers across the path of my loved ones. I thank You now for sending to them the right witness with the right message and the right qualifications at the right time, in Jesus' name.

Angels, go forth now and minister to my family members for they shall be heirs of salvation. Protect them from danger and harm. Protect them from the evil influences of the enemy. Influence them for good in Jesus' name. Set up divine appointments for them with God's laborers.

Precious Holy Spirit, I thank You that You are working right now in the lives of every one of my yet to be saved family members. Convict them of sin, righteousness and judgment. I thank You for revealing to them the reality and goodness of Jesus and for bringing them into the kingdom of God.

Lord, I trust You and I believe Your Word. I thank You that my whole family shall be saved and that we will all stand before Your Throne one day praising and worshipping You. Be glorified in my family in the name of Jesus. AMEN!"

ABOUT THE AUTHOR

Fred Lambert was born the first time in 1960. He was born again in 1984. In the same year he married the love of his life, the beautiful and noble Judy. They have two grown children – Joshua and Hannah, a daughter in-love – Irene, a son in-love – Kevin - five wonderful grandchildren – Joy, Noah, Dylan, Zoe and Elijah.

Fred plays guitar and piano, sings, writes songs and loves to worship. He has recorded three albums. He is the founder of Fred Lambert Ministries, a non-profit international missions organization. He is pastor of the Freie Christengemeinde Wels (Free Christian Church Wels) in Austria where he's lived since 1994. He and Judy are the national directors for Rhema Bible Training College Austria. His favorite color is blue. His favorite ice-cream is pistachio. His favorite food is the world famous "Philly Cheesesteak Hoagie". His favorite holiday is Christmas. His favorite sport is baseball, and his favorite superhero is Jesus!

You can visit Fred at www.fredlambert.net.

A Tax Honesty Primer

Primer

How 67 million Americans have escaped
Congress' largest financial crime
and why your CPA and pastor defend it

David M. Zuniga

W0013842

Other books by David M. Zuniga

This Bloodless Liberty

Fear The People (4th Ed.)

Our First Right

A Republic to Save: Essays in Tactical Civics

Book One: Tactical Civics

Book Two: Mission to America

Tactical Civics[TM] Ready Constitution

Grand Jury Awake

Tactical Civics[TM] High School Edition

His books in progress

Changing America's Mind

Book Three: Engine of Change

Book Four: The Banished Bureaucrat

Book Five: The Greatest Awakening

The Statesman's Manual: A Citizen-Statesman's Guide to Writing and Enacting Legislation Conforming to the Constitution and Supporting the Rule of Law

Dedication

This work is dedicated to those Americans who paid the price in lost wages and sleep; who had their businesses and marriages destroyed, and in some cases served prison time rather than submit to America's largest financial crime, from which the lawless Congress and America's pastors and CPAs make their living. These fighters for Tax Honesty have been called 'tax cheats' and worse. Some have stood on solid research, others on shaky or even preposterous theories.
But all of them have been among the most devoted patriots in our republic.

Contents

Chapter 1

Introduction

I've been a law-abiding Nontaxpayer for over 28 years. I don't fear my employees at the IRS.

This book is neither legal nor tax advice. Americans have the God-given right called freedom of speech; neither corrupt government nor collusive 'tax professionals' can stop us from speaking, or thinking. This book does not incite law-breaking, violence, or even tar-and-feathers for thieves in Congress or their bag-men at IRS.

Congress has long cultivated the IRS to be a lawless, unethical, highly politicized terror agency, as May 2013 news stories reveal. On June 13, 2013 a member of Congress (the IRS's employer) suddenly questioned what its employees were doing, practicing with AR-15 rifles. See the article HERE.

Per Section 7608(a)(1) of the Code, only those IRS operatives engaged in enforcement of Subtitle E (alcohol, tobacco, firearms) are authorized by law to carry any kind of firearm. Hitler's Gestapo could not have done a more preposterous job of probing into Americans' private lives, communications – even their private thoughts and intentions! – as IRS did in its 2015-16 round of scandals. Meanwhile, these criminal operatives party hearty at Taxpayer expense.

Don't take my word for it; watch a video HERE of Tax Honesty spokesman Joe Banister, former IRS Criminal Investigation Division Special Agent at the 2012 Constitutional Sheriffs and Peace Officers Association, explaining to fellow law enforcement personnel how corrupt the Congress' IRS scam is.

Or go to the website of Christian mom, author, and former IRS Fraud Examiner <u>Sherry Peel Jackson</u>, who served two and a half years in prison for blowing the whistle on the criminal nature of the IRS.

This primer is a bit long; I haven't had time to edit this as well as I'd like, but some subjects in life can't be conveyed in sound bites. If you're not a reader, take it in installments.

If reading just isn't your cup of tea, go watch television and stay in the 'fair share' line, but don't complain about America becoming the next Russia. It's *your* fault for financially supporting it, in ignorance.

This Tax Honesty Primer is for Americans like me, who are as mad as hell at the corrupt, brazen Washington D.C. al Qaeda that believes they can do whatever they please, no matter how unconstitutional (illegal) and yet coerce Taxpayers to keep pulling the load like stupid oxen. You're not an ox. Even if you graduated from government schools, you have a brain; it's not illegal to use it.

Living Lawfully – and Free

It doesn't take that many courageous, self-governing citizens to turn the tide of history, even if most people are afraid of their employees in Washington. At least in my own family life and finances, I have worked hard and studied long, to have the liberty that was once America's promise. I live in greater liberty than my grandparents knew. The Internet is the great leveler against corrupt, powerful people who have enslaved working citizens for many generations. The law is on the side of right – on *our* side.

When government becomes as massive and corrupt as Washington D.C. is, the last thing we need is lawless people as a counter-punch; we need rule of law for everyone. If you read this primer, I hope you'll agree to make *honesty* your personal goal. I've read the Tax Code and cases for 26 years, more than five times as long as I studied engineering at university. Two years into my due diligence, I stopped keeping records, filing, and fearing my employees.

2

For over 28 years, I haven't financially supported criminals. I don't worry about today's news cycles or political fights because I don't have a dog in that fight anymore. I don't allow Nancy Pelosi, Mitch McConnell, and all their fellow corrupt scum to skim my checks for their illicit uses.

If you're still trapped in the 'fair share' (of gang rape) line, still getting your reaming every paycheck, then you may hold it against me. Please don't. Like millions of non-filers who are law-abiding Nontaxpayers, I'm happy and relieved that for over two decades I haven't been funding socialist, illegal federal projects, agencies, offices, powers, programs, perks, pork, and regulations...all the things that have Taxpayers wrapped in chains.

Face it: you're paying for your own chains, and you haven't done your homework. Before America becomes the next Red China, why not start doing your due diligence as an American?

A succession of presidents and congresses has made a mockery of what America and liberty once meant. The corruption is defended by most federal judges in America, but it's *still* corruption. I believe that every American must begin to stand against the corruption, and that each citizen has to be convinced of the rightness of his own actions.

As you'll soon see, I also think the vast preponderance of the law is on the side of Tax Honesty, and always has been. You've just been ignorant (not stupid; uninformed), so you've been snookered. Every paycheck.

Tax Honesty has a larger purpose than just allowing us to keep more of what we earn. Congress didn't use *magic* to increase the size and powers of federal Leviathan by over 1000% in just three generations.

Compare the long list of hundreds of departments, powers, agencies, bureaus, and projects that Congress has created, compared to the 17 enumerated, specific powers we granted our federal creature in the Constitution. It's a malignant, never-ending cancer.

As illustrated from the OMB's federal budgets, about 75% of federal expenditures are *illegal.* This means these funds are going to things that are not even reasonably *inferred* from the 17 enumerated powers. Just illegal; for almost 150 years, Congress has become increasingly like every other government on earth: a shakedown and extortion racket.

Still, the problem is created not by the *Taxspenders,* but by the *Taxpayers.* Think about any spoiled brat you ever encountered; the kid is a piece of work, right? But the parents are to blame. That huge, out-of-control government that millions of us love to complain about only exists today because Taxpayers keep sending in trillions!

Legal or illegal expenditures, it doesn't matter; the bureaucrats and terrorists spend it this year, or their department gets less next year. This is the way of all government personnel and programs (yes, even the bloated, bureaucratic, corrupt military machine that Eisenhower warned us about in 1961). Taxpayers are funding *huge* violations of the Constitution, and they need to stop it!

Please stop listening to the phony-baloney, plastic-banana WWF matches that comprise today's news cycles (with the exception of some FOX programming). This political theatre is meant to keep you confused and/or asleep. I include most GOP jingos in that assessment (i.e., Bill O'Reilly, Rush Limbaugh, Sean Hannity) and certainly any 'financial peace' expert who teaches you how to save $995 while letting you continue to be bamboozled by the IRS scam for tens of thousands per year. None of these people will speak plainly about truth, nor will they perform due diligence to report truth.

The real game: those $3,900,000,000,000 need to keep gushing in every year, skimmed off your paychecks. The bad guys want to keep spending and living as they do now, or even better. If you don't like carrying the load, tough. *"It's the law!",* says your CPA and 'financial peace' guru.

Yet every one of them has been sent irrefutable evidence similar to what you will read here. They simply don't want to spoil their great gigs. Even preachers of 'financial peace' refuse to do what Joe Banister and other former IRS whistle-blowers have done: *tell the truth* about the largest terror operation in America, sponsored by the U.S. Congress.

Though they aren't necessarily like him morally, in one sense these consultants are like Bernie Madoff: their income derives from your unwillingness to do your homework. Even if they manage to get free of deep debt, most Americans continue to believe Congress' IRS scam all their lives. *Without ever cracking open a Tax Code.*

This is human nature; it's cause-and-effect. Read Ecclesiastes in the Old Testament; shysters didn't just come up with this at Tammany Hall or in FDR's New Deal era. Corruption is as old as mankind.

Setting aside theories for or against paying 'your fair share', bloated government and corruption are guaranteed as long as Taxpayers keep letting their checks get skimmed by people who lie for a living.

Chapter 2
Earth's Largest Crime Cartel

"Silence can only be equated with fraud where there is a legal or moral duty to speak, or where an inquiry left unanswered would be intentionally misleading. . . We cannot condone this shocking behavior by the IRS. Our revenue system is based on the good faith of the taxpayer and the taxpayers should be able to expect the same from the government in its enforcement and collection activities." U.S. v. Tweel, 550 F.2d 297, 299. See also U.S. v. Prudden, 424 F.2d 1021, 1032; Carmine v. Bowen, 64 A. 932.

Forget the War on Drugs; D.C. is earth's largest crime cartel. In cash equivalent and corrupting power, the present federal revenues take equals over 11,000 major drug cartels operating inside the D.C. beltway. Let that sink in! Yet, for almost three decades I haven't been financially supporting the cartel. Not anymore. After I proved to myself that the Tax Code is perfectly constitutional, I had no problem with the Tax Code. I obey it, but I don't let scammers skim my checks.

Admittedly, being a Texan (no state income tax) and being self-employed, this is much easier for me than for some. But truth is still truth; the law applies equally to every citizen who fights for equal protection under the laws. This is America, not Mexico or China. This primer will explain what I have researched and discovered about Congress' taxation scheme.

You'll see why I came to the conclusions I came to, and why the IRS hasn't touched one dollar in my accounts or one hair on my head in 28 years although I was very vocal with them by certified mail for over a decade (they've been quiet for 17 years now).

I've made enough every year to be a Taxpayer if I wanted to be, but the law doesn't require it of me, so I'm a law-abiding Nontaxpayer. I've owned marked-up copies of the Tax Code, and have enjoyed studying tax law and history for 30 years, since two years before I stopped filing.

I haven't filed IRS forms or paid income taxes in 28 years, after getting nothing but Tax Honesty evasion from the following among our employees at IRS:

Michael Thomas (IRS Austin)

Nancy Sessions (IRS Austin)

Beverly Coogan (IRS San Antonio)

Aaron Hamor (IRS San Antonio)

R.A. Mitchell (IRS Dallas)

C. Sherwood (IRS Dallas)

Grace Metro (IRS Dallas)

Debra K. Hurst (IRS Dallas)

Dennis Parizek (IRS Ogden)

Deborah Egan (IRS Ogden)

Susan Meredith (IRS Fresno)

Teresa Webb (IRS Memphis)

Stephanie Borop (IRS Nashville)

Queen Vaughn (IRS Nashville)

I wrote to them, always by certified mail, asking: "Where is the section of law making me legally liable for keeping records, filing returns, and paying your demands? Some things are called out as taxable activities in the Tax Code; in fact, many activities. But most aren't...including my line of work. So can you show me where the law creates a liability for my own kind of gainful activity, as it does for all those others?"

If you ask such a question, don't hold your breath waiting for an answer. Just like their bosses, my members of Congress whom I contacted, all the IRS operatives listed above have engaged in willful tax honesty evasion, sending one of two bogus non-responses: 1) "we haven't finished our research; we'll get back to you", or 2) "we forwarded your request to the office shown below".

Remember that game from the playground? Hot Potato. In law enforcement, it's called fraud and conspiracy. I refuse to finance more corruption by letting Congress skim my checks. After a decade of being very vocal with them on this point, D.C. al Qaeda has never touched me, my money, or my property.

[They have, however, committed indictable, criminal acts of fraud according to the Texas Penal Code. I'll tell you about that later. Let's go one step at a time.]

Chapter 3

Some People *Are* Made Liable in the Code

Notice I'm not suggesting that there's no law making anyone liable for income tax. Reading the Tax Code, I can find sections that require a person to keep certain records, file certain forms, etc....IF they live and/or work in D.C., Guam, Puerto Rico, or the Northern Mariana Islands. Or if they're involved in manufacture or sale of alcohol, tobacco, or firearms.

Or if they're an officer or employee of the federal government. Or if they're a nonresident alien or a principal of a foreign corporation with income derived from sources within the United States. ...or IF they receive items of taxable income from foreign sources...or foreign mineral income... or income from foreign oil and gas extraction...or income from a foreign controlled corporation as fiduciary agent of the corporation, or from insuring U.S. risks under 26 U.S.C. 953(b)(5). Or...heh...if they receive items of income from maritime (international) trade in opium, cocaine or other controlled substances. [Who the heck would report activities like that?]

Anyway, my point is that Tax Honesty does not maintain that "there's no law!" as some like to caricature Tax Honesty. I simply say that the Tax Code is very specific, and that I do *obey* it, and that I make our federal employees obey it *also*. They use scary letterhead with a little black vulture on it, but letterhead doesn't frighten a person who has a copy of the Tax Code in hand, and knows how to read the English language.

Keep this in mind as you read this book; I am *not* suggesting that nobody owes federal income taxes. But as you will soon see: *you* probably don't.

11

Chapter 4

Financial Crime of Staggering Size

While the first income tax, as already explained, was levied by Lincoln and the 37th Congress during Lincoln's war, <u>Phil Hart's book</u> outlines the history of Congress' IRS scam in the early 20th century. But if the 16th Amendment was passed in 1913, why did it take a generation for most Americans to be snookered into believing it was their civic duty?

It seemed odd to me: although the tax industry apologists and gurus love to claim that the 16th Amendment made everyone liable, the history of tax revenue numbers don't support that assertion. What happened? An entire generation passed before Congress, the tax industry, and government schooling could defraud America's productive population. Describing Walt Disney cartoons featuring Donald Duck and Uncle Scrooge aimed at getting Americans to 'pay their fair share', Amity Schlaes concluded in her book *The Greedy Hand* that plenty of war and government propaganda was needed to finally fool the people.

If you read Phil Hart's book you'll be blood-spittingly furious at the U.S. Congress...and at every tax accountant and attorney you know!

A Financial Crime of Staggering Size

The federal government can lawfully exercise only the 17 powers specifically enumerated to it in Article I Section 8. This is the most basic American civics. To exercise its lawful powers, Congress must collect taxes, fine; we agree. But depending on how fat an imperial 'force projection' military one assumes, the total *lawful* powers of federal government would require $400-$800 billion annually to fund. Yet, Congress is now collecting over $3.9 *trillion* annually, with almost half of that being taken from individuals as income taxes. So before listening to guru sites like 'Quatloos' assertions about Tax Honesty proponents being cheaters, liars, and crooks, consider the prior question: who is committing *real* crimes here? Before asking whether it's illegal or immoral for an individual to refuse to pay tribute to the IRS – first ask, what is Congress doing with the funds that it *already* collects? Based on the black-letter U.S. Constitution, about 75% of the powers that federal government currently exercises is illegal according to Article I Section 8, so why should citizens give them even *more?*

To put it another way: If every Taxpayer – even those relative few who engage in taxable activities stipulated in the Tax Code – stopped paying income taxes tomorrow, the federal government would *still* be collecting three times the revenues required to fund the *lawful* activities of federal government according to the Constitution.

In other words, Congress is running a $2.9 trillion per year crime cartel, yet the defenders of today's tax industry scam want you to believe that law-abiding Nontaxpayers are the real criminals, just because we refuse to give the tax industry mafia a few thousand dollars more each year to feed their habit?

The principle in economics called *moral hazard* holds that if enough people are put under a massive financial burden, the burden will not be felt by each one carrying the burden. If you have a huge pork project, spread it out over enough victims and they'll never feel it.

Try to grasp the depth of communism in our republic today. Agencies, bureaus, departments, programs and projects – often completely invisible and unaccountable to the public, and often being paid to literal mafia figures (as criminologist Donald Cressey reported in his 1969 book Theft of The Nation, but no one listened) and to recipients who are foreign individuals and companies – a clear violation of the U.S. Constitution.

To grasp the sheer scale of the predator/parasite load on your back, there are over 20 million public employees, plus over 50 million truly parasitic citizens and non-citizens drawing their sustenance off of the American taxpayer. This does not include another 50+ million on some government benefits.

In other words, to put the numbers in perspective, productive America is presently carrying the equivalent of the entire populations of Albania, Bahrain, Costa Rica, Croatia, Denmark, Estonia, Finland, Ireland, Jamaica, Kuwait, Lithuania, Mauritania, Mongolia, New Zealand, Norway, Panama, Slovakia, Slovenia, and Uruguay on their backs!

There's an even *more* sinister aspect to Congress' organized crimes: it owes more than *$170 trillion* in unfunded liabilities for its illegal socialist activities: Social Security, Medicare, Medicaid, Federal Unemployment Compensation, and prescription drugs – not to mention interest on the national debt and past war expenditures.

Please understand how truly bankrupt Congress is. It could decide to tax 100% of everything we make, and end all government operations, to magically apply the entire U.S. Gross Domestic Product to paying off Congress' gargantuan credit card debt. It would still take *over eight years* to pay off the debt, but of course all Americans would have died of exposure and hunger long before then.

Of course that's too real, so with its FED printing cartel, Congress perennially kicks the can down the road. It will simply continue to print worthless Monopoly money until the music stops – or at least until the American People finally blow the whistle on the largest financial fraud in human history.

AmericaAgain! Trust and TACTICAL CIVICS™

But by the grace of God, we finally have the truth; and now we have a lawful, peaceful, long-term solution: be a member of AmericaAgain! and join or launch a TACTICAL CIVICS™ chapter in your county.

For the first time, We The People can arrest organized crime in Congress. Far beyond Tax Honesty, the American people require a *law enforcement* mechanism to indict, try and convict members of Congress who flaunt the Supreme Law.

The U.S. Constitution is the highest law in America, and must be obeyed!

We can't wait for corrupt government to fix itself; that's not how organized crime operates and it's *definitely* not how parasites operate on the backs of their hosts.

We The People are the only human power above the U.S. Constitution, to assure that our public servants obey it. This is the purpose of the Indictment Engine™, of training Grand Jury members, of restoring our Militias in every American county, and of the other aspects of the responsible new way of life called <u>TACTICAL CIVICS</u>™.

Chapter 5

Not a Position, Theory, or Belief

Every critical point I make here in *A Tax Honesty Primer* is a citation of primary sources: the rulings of the U.S. Supreme Court, citations from the *Internal Revenue Code, Code of Federal Regulations, Internal Revenue Manual, Black's Law Dictionary,* and *Sutherland's Rules of Statutory Construction.*

You won't find any theories or my 'beliefs' in this Tax Honesty Primer. You'll find citations of those authorities listed above, and also names and an on-the-record statement from former IRS agents, attorneys, auditors, an IRS Commissioner, and the only official Historian of the IRS in the agency's history.

A few housekeeping points

Before we go into the red-pill adventure in the Tax Code, cases, and supporting evidence and rulings I'll chase off cockroaches and lazy web-surfers with a few points of housekeeping:

Point #1. Tax Honesty is the opposite of 'tax protesting'; it's responsible citizenship, neither anti-government nor anti-tax. Rather, Tax Honesty is anti-*corruption* and anti-*terrorist.*

Point #2. As a corollary to Point #1, we all agree that lawful taxation is necessary to fund the lawful functions of government.

Point #3. Tax-theory gurus will keep being convicted for selling loopy theories, but Tax Honesty doesn't support tax-protest theories, theories about the 16th Amendment, theories like 'wages aren't income', or Fifth Amendment rights theories. Nontaxpayers must not take 'positions' or seek to do away with the Tax Code or the IRS. As I see it, Tax Honesty supports the Federal Tax Code as written.

Point #4. You can find in-depth treatment of specific issues at two linked research sites: <u>WhatIsTaxed</u> focuses on data mining the Tax Code and federal regulations; <u>Synaptic Sparks</u> explains the legal principles of Tax Honesty.

Point #5. If you work in the tax industry (government or private-sector) and want to leave the Axis of Evil, I'm happy to answer your e-mails but don't e-mail to debate me. You're defending a scam and I took the red pill. Go pound sand.

Your threat *"I'll visit you in prison!"* is ludicrous; of 67 million non-filers, fewer than 200 are even recommended for indictment by IRS annually and they're people who: 1) demand refunds, 2) file and sign things but then refuse to pay, or 3) follow wacky theories.

IRS recommends *eight times* as many filers for indictment each year, as non-filers. So with 67 million non-filers to 115 million filers, that means you'll visit four times more filer friends in prison for each non-filer there. CPA, learn how your profession has slumped towards Gomorrah in Mike Brewster's book <u>*Unaccountable: How the Accounting Profession Forfeited a Public Trust.*</u> If you intend to continue holding clients down while IRS does bad things to them, don't delude yourself that you're a professional performing a needed service. That's nonsense.

The annual Tax Terror Season

If you're still a Taxpayer, you're terrorized by your employees at IRS because they drag out a few high-profile 'tax cheat' trophies every Tax Terror Season (Jan 1- Apr 15). It's the same idea your CPA or tax preparer uses when they repeat the death-and-taxes line; the tax industry plays good cop to IRS's bad cop. Your heart pounds, you borrow the money for the next IRS payment, your CPA makes his Bentley payment, and you trudge ahead in the 'fair share' line.

Dying Communism and 'tax professionals' in the tar pit

According to former IRS Fraud Examiner Sherry Peel (later a Tax Honesty spokeswoman), there were 67 million non-filers as of 2005 compared with 'only' 30 million non-filers by Commissioner Rosotti's 1998 estimate; an astounding growth rate. With an estimated 124 million filers, at least one in three Americans is no longer underwriting the corrupt Congress' bailout and check-skimming machine.

As James Davidson and Lord William Rees-Mogg predicted ten years ago in their book *The Sovereign Individual* – the internet is making bureaucratic, redistributionist governments unsustainable; the dinosaurs are in the tar-pit. Today's financial news signifies the struggle for survival between Taxpayers and Taxspenders; this battle reached critical mass in The Age of Obama.

In the Bush II era, we saw textbook fascism: massive expansion of the police state and military, restrictions on liberty of travel, eavesdropping on our calls and emails, and more. During the 8-year Obamanation, we saw textbook communism: destruction of private property, national-ization of major industries, and crippling new regulation and taxation to make the slaves pay for their own chains. With open communism returning to Congress now as in the 1930s, this is a critical phase in modern history: the D.C. al Qaeda will attempt to stay alive and grow like cancer into every area of life where it doesn't already control.

Even as tens of millions of Americans become Nontaxpayers, millions of Taxpayers are going broke, live under IRS duress or payment plans, and curse life in America. *This is just wrong.* It's not only injustice; it's 'professionals' abetting corruption; helping Congress obscure the real issues and appealing to collusive federal judges' rulings about 'frivolous tax protestors'.

They know that, like those collusive judges, this is about their careers continuing on your back. You're their pack-mule; their free lunch. Their next payment for the high-rise office and the Cancun condo. This isn't even about law for them; it's all about those trillions of dollars per year. Increasingly in the Age of Obamanation, Taxpayers realized this.

It's about time! Yes, something is happening in America – and around the world. *Pushback.* Here in the American republic, the Ron Paul

Revolution, TEA Party movement, heated battle about the government's socialist takeover of healthcare and legalizing sexual perversion as 'marriage', and finally the election of Donald Trump – are all facets of a growing trend against Leviathan.

The Internet is liberating citizens to dig up corruption; to unearth who did what in history. To bring the best lights we have to shine on the money-trail. The parasite sector will now be put on defense, at long last. They won't like it. Well, *tough*.

Since his election, Obama made no attempt to hide his socialist plan, buying and controlling corporate giants using your tax dollars whether you agree or not. While Trump is delivering some relief, presidents have great power for evil but little power to make lasting improvements.

This Leviathan push will not abate on its own; every free-rider in every housing project, welfare line, illegal alien safe house, military retirement plan, legal and accounting office or seminar room, and in every congressman's and senator's lair, every meeting of ACORN or MoveOn.org…these are the takers. Even much of the bloated American military machine is all about a cushy life at Taxpayer expense.

The poor Taxpayers are finally at the breaking point…and willing to do some homework. That's what this booklet is all about; my effort to help you avoid the loopy theorist sites form *both* sides of the Tax Honesty war. Yes, this is a civil war of sorts; the fight for your checking account. You against them; taxpayer against taxspender and all the shills of the taxspender such as the tax preparation industry and academia.

As the American people take a stand against organized crime operating as government, the obvious first step is to cut its supply line.

Chapter 6

No Law Makes Most Americans Liable

Does that statement sound unbelievable? It's been asserted and proven beyond reasonable doubt to juries across America over two decades:

Thomas Reeves of Paducah, KY made the same assertion in 1988; the jury *acquitted him*. Franklin Sanders and (16) co-defendants in the Memphis area made the same assertion in 1991; the jury *acquitted them*. Gabriel Scott of Fairbanks, AK made the same assertion in 1992; the jury *acquitted him*. Lloyd Long of Chattanooga, TN made the same assertion in 1993; the jury *acquitted him*. Frederick and Christopher Allnut of Baltimore, MD made the same assertion in 1996; the jury *acquitted them*. Gaylon Harrell of Logan County, IL made the same assertion in 2000; the jury *acquitted him*. Donald Fecay of Detroit, MI made the same assertion in 2001; the jury *acquitted him*. Vernice Kuglin of Memphis, TN made the same assertion in 2003; the jury *acquitted her*. Dr. Lois Somerville of Lake Mary, FL made the same assertion in 2003; U.S. District Judge Patricia C. Fawsett *acquitted her*. Former Treasury Department CID agent Joe Banister made the same assertion in 2005; the jury *acquitted him*. Attorney Thomas Cryer of Shreveport, LA made the same assertion in 2007; the jury *acquitted him*.

Every case stands on its own fact situations, of course; but a person also shouldn't listen to freeloaders who put a guilt trip on those who don't file, saying *"Nontaxpayers don't pay their fair share for roads, schools, and trash pickup!"* Learn what all those jurors learned: those things are *not* funded by federal tax revenues. You're being extorted and raped. Start reading!

Cognitive Dissonance and America's Parasite Sector

Ask anyone who invested with Ponzi-scheme huckster Bernard Madoff: the very nature of successful fraud is that it does actually defraud. The mark actually believes the fraudster, sometimes for many years. So this will be weirder than hearing that your spouse of 25 years has been cheating on you since your wedding night...stranger than finding out that your best friend is an axe-murderer.

Cognitive dissonance is what happens when everything you ever knew about something is turned upside down. You may get light-headed and confused; that's normal. When you start considering doing something about it, if you're not very courageous you may get anxiety attacks and lose sleep. That's normal too.

Upton Sinclair said, *"It is difficult to get a man to understand something when his salary depends upon his not understanding it."* Your CPA may refuse to discuss Tax Honesty, threatening, "I'll see you in prison!". He doesn't want his professional career exposed as corrupt; what do you *expect* him to say?

The defenders of 'pay your taxes' are legion. Congress' IRS scam is almost impossible to expose because it feeds a massive parasite population that you've likely never considered. Most of us produce something of use to others, or we fix things, or grow things, or sell useful stuff. But today, there are literally tens of millions of parasite-sector Americans:

Corrupt politicians including federal judges...their bloated staffs and other bureaucrats...thousands of gov't contractors employing millions of Americans...IRS employees...large accounting firms and individual accountants...tax law firms and their employees...tax software companies...tax training (seminar & publishing) companies...tax preparation services...university endowments in tax law & accounting...tax-deferred investment groups...tax-shelter mutual funds...the tax shelter real estate sector...equipment, vehicle, and aircraft leasing companies...manufacturers and vendors of all depreciable equipment...IRS workout services that advertise "we're former IRS agents"...and the two really big Kahunas: America's mortgage industry, and America's non-profit industry, both religious and secular.

You never considered the connection between all those industries and Congress' IRS crime cartel, but now you know why you hear *"pay your taxes"* and *"render unto Caesar"* from counselors who have enjoyed great public trust and respect. If they run from Tax Honesty, they don't deserve that trust and respect. They have chosen a parasitic life.

In an interview in the May 25, 1956 issue of *U.S. News & World Report,* IRS Commissioner T. Coleman Andrews said, *"There is a veritable army of people, organizations and businesses with a powerful vested interest in keeping the noses of the rest of us to the grindstone...let no one underestimate the power of the* [tax industry]." There was *one* honest Commissioner of the IRS, anyway.

Loopy Tax Protestor Gurus vs. Crooked Tax Industry Gurus

Let me say again: this is not legal or tax advice. Learn as you read, and don't let this be all you read. Take everything with a grain of salt until you test statements against one another, and against the law as written.

With respect to the income tax, law means the actual words of the Tax Code; nothing else is law. Not an IRS letter or demand, and not an IRS pamphlet or flyer about 'your rights as a Taxpayer'. Those are P.R. eyewash from an administrative branch agency; the stimulus gang's bag men. IRS publications have *zero* legal weight.

Under our rule of law everyone – including IRS employees – must obey the law. Remember that next time your employees try to terrorize you. Incidentally, I also don't put much stock in 'tax protestor' theories and those who peddle them. As I did my research over the years, I found a great deal of hokum and snake-oil in the early Tax Honesty movement, what was probably accurately termed 'tax protesting'.

I found a gazillion theories: twisting some quote or ruling out of context...making up theories about capitalization...about admiralty law... about the UCC...about wages not being income...about U.S. citizenship being of the devil...about the 16th Amendment never being properly ratified (maybe not, but it's immaterial)...about the Tax Code being unconstitutional...about Section 861 being a secret silver bullet...blah blah. I'll stick to the law as written; rulings that make sense in context.

I'll follow that money trail to see how Leviathan did what it has done. As an engineer, I like to see things make sense (you know, Occam's Razor and all that). When you reach the citations of U.S. Supreme Court rulings below, and you're trying to decide who has more clout in the system, keep this section of the Internal Revenue Manual in mind:

Internal Revenue Manual 4.10.7.2.9.8

Importance of Court Decisions

A case decided by the U.S. Supreme Court becomes the law of the land and takes precedence over decisions of lower courts. The Internal Revenue Service must follow Supreme Court decisions. For examiners, Supreme Court decisions have the same weight as the Code.

So, the U.S. Supreme Court trumps the IRS. Remember that as you read this primer or anything sent to you by the IRS.

AAAaugh!! I can't find my socks!!!

Whether you're a filer or non-filer, you should own a current copy of the Tax Code. Don't waste hundreds of hours being dragged by the nose through Congress' maze of smoke and mirrors; instead, do as I did:

a) bought the latest IRC; I use <u>Thomson Reuters' single-volume edition</u>.

b) bought a highlighter and a set of color-coded plastic index tabs

c) went through the whole book and found only (124) lines in the 9,500-page Code that specifically indicate activities imposing a legal duty to keep records, file, and pay. I highlighted and tabbed those sections.

Don't believe the tax industry line about how "huge and confusing" the Tax Code is. Nonsense; they just want you to stay scared and confused.

Here's a fitting analogy. When Smith wants to buy some new socks from Sears, does he fall on the floor in a tearful heap, wailing, *"Aaaaauuuugh!! That confounded 10,000-page catalog!! No American can understand it!! Even the people who wrote it can't give me a straight answer! It's HUGE!! Waaaaahh!!"* ?

Of course not; that would be very silly. Smith just opens the catalog or the simple website to the page for men's socks, orders what he needs, and treats the gazillions of other things in the huge catalog or website as if they don't exist. Well, it's the same thing with laws, including the Tax Code. If a law doesn't apply to who you are or what you do, then you can treat that law as though it doesn't exist.

To put it another way: do you worry about not obeying Federal Aviation Regulations for Airframe & Powerplant Mechanics? No. Unless you're an airframe and powerplant mechanic working on aircraft that fall within the regulatory aegis of the FAA. Every other American treats those federal codes as if they don't exist.

The same is true for federal laws and regulations concerning nuclear power plant operators, or producers of explosives or distillers and sellers of alcohol, or what-have you. If a law pertains to you, obey it; but you can safely ignore any law if it doesn't pertain to you.

As you'll see the U.S. Supreme Court ruling repeatedly below, and the Internal Revenue Manual demanding of every IRS employee below – laws of taxation must be clear, and the person from whom a tax is sought must be shown in *specific language* to be taxable. Everyone else can just leave the big, fat book aside; it doesn't apply to them.

My CPAs over the years, if they had been competent and honest, should have known that it never had applied to me. But most in 'the system' won't tell you that because they're like nerds with pocket protectors standing in every aisle at Sears. Huge catalog in hand, their career is showing you what page to look on so you can buy your socks. If you figure out the game, they're out of work. So don't expect them to support Tax Honesty. We're all human, and even pirates need to eat.

Like all laws, the Tax Code applies only to certain subjects

As you'll see presently, well-settled law including U.S. Supreme Court rulings over a century hold that when a tax law lists some things as taxable, then things *not* listed are *not* taxable. As I read the citations below, according to the U.S. Supreme Court, the law must *specifically* point out what activities and situations are taxable.

We have no Caesars

See if you agree: with your own copy of the law marked up to show specifically listed taxable activities, you can confirm what the Tax Code requires of a 'taxpayer'; who the law makes a 'taxpayer' – versus what your CPA, H&R Block guy, an IRS employee, or tax dishonesty guru Dan Evans may claim. A common response from those in the system when Tax Honesty arises is, *"render unto Caesar!"*.

Really? Obviously we're not ancient Rome. Americans are not ruled by Caesars but by *rule of law*. That means government is ruled by our federal and State Constitutions and We The People are ruled by laws and regulations *only* to the extent that *they* obey those constitutions.

The Internal Revenue Code (26 USC) is the codification of the statutes that establish a legal duty for certain people to keep records, file forms, and pay income tax...but only those people whose activities or situations meet the taxing provisions in the Code, according to the U.S. Supreme Court, and Black's Law Dictionary, and Sutherland's Rules of Statutory Construction, as you will see below.

Thus, a person who meets those Tax Code provisions specifically called out in law, but refuses to pay the taxes stipulated is properly called a tax evader. But anyone *not* made liable in the specific language of the Tax Code is free to be a Nontaxpayer, legally free to ignore that law just as he ignores all other law codes that don't apply to him.

IRS Whistleblowers

The Code of Ethics for Government Service requires any government employee or official who finds evidence of a government violation of law to report the violation, not to cover it up or participate as a conspirator, which is what IRS employees do daily. A government official or employee who violates laws is not to be obeyed, but reported for those violations and indicted where applicable.

The IRS has had a few honest and courageous employees over the years. In her sworn testimony before the Senate Finance Committee in 1997, Shelley L. Davis, the only official IRS Historian in the history of that agency, said the IRS is deeply corrupt; see her article in Appendix A.

Former IRS employees have learned the truth about Congress' IRS scam, left the agency and are now spokesmen for Tax Honesty including Treasury and CID agent Joe Banister, IRS agents Clifton Beale and John Turner, IRS fraud examiner Sherry Jackson, IRS attorney Paul Chappell, and IRS auditor Matthew McErlean.

In a 1956 interview for U.S. News & World Report, IRS Commissioner Andrews said, *"I don't like the income tax...every time we talk about these taxes we get the idea of 'from each according to his capacity and to each according to his needs.' That's socialism! It's written into the Communist Manifesto...Maybe we ought to see that everybody who gets a tax return receives...a Communist Manifesto with it, so he can see what's happening to him."*

The heart of the trap: "Everybody has to pay their taxes!"

I'm not a tax lawyer, CPA, tax accountant, nor do I offer legal or tax advice. I'm a follower of Christ first, a Texan second and an American third. We have the God-given right to speak about our rights and duties for self-government; the government and tax industry practitioners and terrorists can't restrict that right.

Perhaps your HR manager, CPA, or tax preparer has shown you the Tax Code section, *"...every individual having for the taxable year..."* and suggests that this means every person that makes money, saying everybody has to pay 'their' taxes.

Nonsense. I do have to pay 'my taxes' if that means every sales tax, excise tax, property tax, import duty, etc... that I owe by law. But I don't have to pay 'my taxes' as defined by a fraudulent, mercenary tax industry but not found in law. The tax industry and online gurus who inveigh against Tax Honesty love to peddle the lie that the Tax Code reads like the Revenue Act of 1894:

There shall be assessed, levied, collected, and paid annually upon the gains, profits, and income received in the preceding calendar year by every citizen of the United States…from any profession, trade, employment, or vocation carried on in the United States or elsewhere, or from any other source whatsoever, a tax.

Can't be any more all-encompassing than that, right? If everybody just owed a tax, the whole Tax Code would always have been one paragraph long, right? Everybody has to pay. But that's an extortionist's lie, and you can't build a whole industry including many college and university departments and publishing houses on such a simple tax.

As Phil Hart explains in his book, the present income tax scheme was devised by a very sneaky Congress after the Supreme Court ruled that the language above was unconstitutional (in fact, the court forced Congress to return what it had collected from the people under the 1894 act). To hide the truth – very few occupations trigger a Tax Code liability section – the crooks in Congress made the Tax Code increasingly large and complex.

Still, beneath ten thousand pages of gobbledygook, the Code is as it always was: very limited in its scope, just as the framers meant internal taxation to be. As the US Supreme Court has repeatedly ruled, it only applies to activities *specifically* called out in the law; to persons having taxable income. Persons made liable for an income tax in the Code; persons defined in Section 7701(a)14 as Taxpayers.

Are income taxes voluntary?

How could so many people be so blind to fraud and theft of this magnitude? Well, in the first place, I began to realize (as I showed you) how many industries and careers are in cahoots pushing the propaganda. Parasites need to eat, just like productive people do.

The top ranks of media are in league with friends in Congress; the lower ranks are terrorized of being ruined by IRS. So it makes sense that a lot of people insist that everyone paying income taxes is a legal duty.

But some people maintain that income taxes are voluntary, basing their theory on snippets of the ruling in the 1960 Flora case: *'Our system of taxation is based upon voluntary assessment and payment, not upon distraint.'* Flora v. United States, 362 U.S. 176 (1960).

Wait a sec, now...what does that ruling mean? I think those who claim that all income tax is voluntary are reading too much into *Flora*. Obviously, for anyone whose activities are specifically listed in the Tax Code, paying income taxes is *not* voluntary.

Still, I was flabbergasted when I realized what the court's ruling in Flora *did* mean: because I had no legal duty according to the Tax Code, for 20 years I really had been volunteering; self-assessing and signing up as 'taxpayer' just because I was defrauded and terrorized by Congress and the tax industry. I have never engaged in any activity specifically called out in the Tax Code. I just volunteered out of ignorance and terror. Just as you have always done.

As I will reiterate often in this primer: some activities *are* listed in the Code as having a legal duty to keep records, file, and pay. I'm not one of those who says, "there's no law for any American to pay income taxes". Nonsense; in this booklet I list what the Tax Code stipulates as activities, occupations, or domicile classes specifically making a person liable for keeping records, filing forms, and paying a tax.

But *my* gainful activities aren't listed anywhere; so for two decades, I was just self-assessing and signing promissory documents under penalty of perjury without ever having even seen a copy of the Code, much less having read it or researched it. I was scammed by Congress, the IRS, and the parasitic tax industry including my CPAs over the years. I was just doing what everybody else did.

I was ignorant, like Bernie Madoff's victims, for decades.

The court didn't say in *Flora* that even if by law I don't owe a tax, but everybody makes me think I do, that once I self-assess, sign under penalty of perjury, and mail the tax return, I then owe what I promise anyway! That would be fraud, extortion, and entrapment.

Okay...so what is going on with you filers? Is it government fraud and entrapment for 115 million people to file things without looking into the Tax Code even the least bit? Is it government fraud and entrapment for a Taxpayer to let the state and federal Leviathan skim 40% of his livelihood, without seeing if he ever owed it by law?

Well, okay; technically it's extortion and racketeering. But the larger aspect of this scam is that *you,* a Taxpayer, have failed to perform due diligence as a free, self-governing citizen under our American system of popular sovereignty. Call it ignorance, apathy, or state-sponsored terror.

There are over 67 million of us who are no longer afraid of the hired help, even if they try to frighten us with the little black vulture letterhead and envelope with the cleverly-designed black bar on the fringe...what a tricky, subliminal terror tactic, that black bar! And on you 115 million terror victims still in the IRS gulag, those black branding items work beautifully. They instill FEAR.

But we law-abiding Nontaxpayers don't have CPAs telling us what we "must do by law" so they can keep their cushy careers. Unless they are committing immoral or illegal acts, no free people can possibly live in fear of their public servants yet honestly call themselves free. I helped destroy our Constitutional Republic as an ignorant filer funding criminals for 20 years; so I felt it my duty after years of research, to begin writing and editing this Tax Honesty Primer first as a website and now many years later a booklet, to atone for my 20 years of abdication.

Now, I teach my fellow Americans in all 50 states, how this republic of sovereign States and sovereign People was transformed into a socialist empire of mobsters at the federal, state, county, city, and school board levels, now joined by a huge parasitic segment within the private sector and illegal aliens as well. If you read Thomas DiLorenzo's 2012 book Organized Crime, or many others by Peter Schweizer or Tom Fitton, and you will learn how criminal and *criminogenic* our 'public servants' have become. It's chilling – and all funded by you, Taxpayer.

So what made me a Taxpayer all those years?

First I had to ask myself: was I a Taxpayer? That may seem like a silly question, but it's the first critical lynch-pin upon which Congress had been hanging my checkbook for 20 years. The Internal Revenue Code defines taxpayer as "any person subject to any internal revenue tax" at 26 USC 7701(a)14, and as "any person subject to a tax under the applicable revenue law" at 26 USC 1313(b).

Okay, but I could never find a section of the Code making me subject to the tax. After over a dozen demands, all of those IRS employees listed by name above refused to supply me with any part of the Code showing a section of law establishing a legal duty in the Code for me or almost anybody else, for that matter.

The 'Taxable Income' position

Some books and websites teach the 'taxable income' line of inquiry, and in fact that line of reasoning was what led former IRS CID agent Joe Banister to leave the IRS.

But I didn't want to play Congress' semantic games: taxable income is defined in terms of "adjusted gross income" in Section 63... "adjusted gross income" is defined in terms of a "taxpayer" in Section 62a...and Section 6012(a) reads, *"Returns with respect to income taxes under subtitle A shall be made by . . . every individual having for the taxable year gross income,"* etc. "Individual" is defined in the regulations...and to have a "taxable year" one must be not only an "individual", but a "taxpayer" according to Section 441(b)(1).

Boy howdy; the whole thing is a spaghetti-bowl maze! Which makes sense; corrupt members of Congress keep trillions coming in every year by rendering the law ever more confusing to the target until he just gives up, self-assesses like the neighbors do, and pays up.

I went back to looking for who is a Taxpayer; where does the law impose a legal duty on me where I live, doing what I do? Why wouldn't IRS employees just show me *that?* Well, *because it doesn't exist.*

26USC A(1)(A)(I)(1)...the favorite semantic trap

Most HR managers make a very short discussion out of it; they trot out the very first sentence in the body of the Tax Code...Subtitle A, Chapter 1, Subchapter A, Part I, Section 1: *"There is hereby imposed on the taxable income of every married individual..."*.

Well, that sure was easy. Everybody owes 'their' taxes, right? No; remember, the Supreme Court ruled that a universal tax is unconstitutional. Over a century ago, the Supreme Court made the corrupt Congress return what it had sucked in under the unconstitutional universal (everybody owes) taxing language. The snakes had to find a different path to your wallet; they did so with help from their partners in accounting, law, and tax preparation.

They did it by adding miles of convoluted word games so that no sane person would try to run the Tax Code maze on his own. For instance, this word 'individual' is an interesting example of fraudulent drafting. Congress pulled this semantic trick because definitions in laws can have a very different meaning from what the same word means in regular conversation. So take another step down the rabbit hole to see how Congress appears to be taxing everyone, while not actually doing that.

If they can use a trick word in just the right place, they won't get their hand slapped again by the Supreme Court. So the Tax Code right up front says that every individual has a tax imposed; and how does Congress define the word individual in the Tax Code? Hmm... *It doesn't*. But the Federal Regulations *do* define individual:

26 CFR 1.1441-1

Requirement for deduction and withholding of tax on payments to foreign persons.

(c) Definitions (3) Individual.

(i) Alien individual. The term alien individual means an individual who is not a citizen...

(ii) Nonresident alien individual. The term nonresident alien individual means a person described in section 7701(b)(1)(B), an alien individual who is...

Notice, it's all just *aliens.* It only talks about *foreign* persons. You may say, *"Don't look there, you ninny; that says 'foreign persons' in the heading".* I know that, but find any *other* place in the Tax Code or Federal Regulations that defines individual. It doesn't exist!

That's just one way to write a law so that it's not unconstitutional, yet you can still hook a great many fish. You have to hand it to those bent multi-millionaires in Congress, they're wily little suckers.

Again, let me make it clear: I didn't need this word-game stuff to prove to myself beyond reasonable doubt that I was never a Taxpayer except by being defrauded into self-assessing and signing up for IRS extortion. It's a simple scam: all those years, as I *self*-assessed and signed, I became what I claimed about myself *under penalty of perjury.*

The law didn't do it to me; my own ignorance and signature made me a 'Taxpayer' as I self-assessed and signed that return without ever having even seen a copy of the Tax Code!

I used search engines on the Tax Code and Federal Regulations. It was easy online to do a Boolean word search for *individual* in the text of the Tax Code. I used the government's own websites and I also made use of http://www.whatistaxed.com/ for my data mining exercise.

Who must provide Form W-4 or W-9?

I've asked IRS a dozen times where the Code says that I must, by law, file returns. The law and their operations manual stipulate that they *must* give me a meaningful answer, not their PR hooey. Yet over 10 years (I haven't heard from them in 17 years) they gave me nothing but evasion, which in themselves are violations of their operating rules in their IRM.

Since they refused to respond, I told them to pound sand every time they bothered me, and eventually they stopped.

I was also asked over the years: which payors are required by law to obtain a W-4, W-9, or a TIN? Well, the only place I have found so far is 26 CFR...Title 26 of the Code of Federal Regulations. Who has a legal duty to furnish a number in response to such a request?

26 CFR 301.6109-1

(c) If the person making the return, statement, or other document does not know the taxpayer identifying number of the other person, and such other person is one that is described in paragraph (b)(2)(i), (ii), (iii), or (vi) of this section, such person must request the other person's number. The request should state that the identifying number is required to be furnished under authority of law.

(b)(2)(i): A foreign person that has income...

(b)(2)(ii): A foreign person that has a U.S. office or...

(b)(2)(iii): A nonresident alien treated as a resident...

(b)(2)(vi): A foreign person that furnishes a withholding certificate...

Notice something familiar? There it is again; only *foreign* persons.

The Rabbit-Trails Go On Forever

These are just a few semantic traps along the rational trail from Tax Code A(1)A(I)(1) onward. Following such trails always left me stuck right about at 'taxable income' or at 'gross income'...going in a circle.

Sneaky, sneaky! Congress and the complicit parasite sector makes it appear that *everybody* has to pay, but it's a huge Bernie Madoff fraud.

Again, remember: when Congress tried that (universal tax language) in 1894, the high court slapped their hand. So again, I knew that 'everybody has to pay' doesn't meet the Constitution's tests for apportionment and uniformity. The U.S. Supreme Court says they can't do that...so *the law does not say that everybody has to pay.*

The semantic traps are built very carefully, to make work for the tax preparation industry, and to confuse Taxpayers. I wanted all possible evidentiary trails played out to their conclusions; so out of morbid

34

curiosity (and sheer terror, in the early years) I still followed *all* the Tax Code rabbit-trails. I searched every Tax Honesty website I could find, many of which don't exist anymore, and most of which were just loopy. I read every Tax Honesty book I could find; similarly, I found most of them to be loopy, but a few were good. I love Phil Hart's book, and several of those that were published by the late Otto Skinner.

I read through the http://www.whatistaxed.com/ data-mining site and the excellent http://www.synapticsparks.info/ website. I walked through the 'gross income' bunny-trail, the 'definition of individual' bunny trail, the Section 861 bunny trail. There are exhaustive analyses (in every sense of the term) on these websites. Synaptic Sparks is particularly comprehensive, and highly recommended.

Busting the Ponzi Scheme

As I'll show shortly, the U.S. Supreme Court has reiterated that if some lines of work *are* listed in a tax law, then a citizen is free unless his line of work is *also* found specifically listed in the Tax Code, in clear language. Tax law must be clear; when it isn't clear and the government can't provide the law behind its actions or demands, the benefit of the doubt goes to the citizen.

This is well-settled law, regardless what Dan Evans may say.

Evans is a Philadelphia lawyer; a self-proclaimed Internet authority or 'de-bunker' of Tax Honesty. Evans rests his entire position on the fact that judges have ruled against several Tax Honesty 'gurus' as he calls them. But there are four problems with Mr. Evans' hokum:

First, regardless how many federal judges might rule in favor of their own paychecks over yours, the law is on the side of citizens and against the IRS scam (read the Supreme Court rulings and other cites below).

Second, of the more than 67 million non-filers, 99.99% of all non-filers are never indicted, much less convicted of anything trumped up by IRS. Just because Dan Evans finds fewer than a half-dozen high-profile trophy convictions per year, doesn't negate 67 million others living free!

Actually, 67 million was a 2005 estimate by a former IRS fraud examiner who became a Tax Honesty whistleblower; some estimates in 2013-14 were that as many as half of all Americans were no longer filing.

Third, just because judges in 1830s America said that a Black slave had to be returned to his 'master', or judges in 1930s Germany said that Jews had to stay in their concentration camps, didn't place those judges on the side of right. Yet, at least those evil judges had law on their side; these do not, as we will see in U.S. Supreme Court rulings below.

Fourth, the favorite tactic of Evans and his two or three comrades who commented regularly on his website was to cast personal aspersions in the manner of kindergarten pugilists who have no game. Their prime argument was *ad hominem* characterization of those whom they oppose in a puerile, petulant style. Name-calling is hardly convincing evidence that Mr. Quatloos is on the side of right. And repeatedly saying, "you will lose!" is equally unconvincing, in an age where Congress clearly has no scruples about violating the highest law in America, hundreds of times per day. So much for the Philadelphia lawyer.

It's not illegal to stop being Bernie Madoff's victim

The rulings I will outline below are well-settled, standing law. I obey the law, and I take comfort in these well-settled principles of how to interpret tax law when dealing with administrative agency operatives.

Visceral fear is the constant companion of all terror victims. Although it's scary at first, Tax Honesty is also profoundly liberating. Following the money and reading the well-settled law brought me clarity and, after a few years, brought me peace as well. It took years to come to grips with the reality that I was a terror victim, scammed by a large parasite population, public and private, all my working life. I knew that the non-productive, parasitic professions and industries were getting to be more popular and ever-larger, while the productive crafts, trades, and learned fields were shrinking. I know who the crooks are now.

As it was for victims of the Bernie Madoff Ponzi scheme – it always looks obvious after you solve the crime. Out of us 67 million non-filers, maybe 20-30 million of us are true, law-abiding Nontaxpayers. Maybe even fewer; I don't care. I do know that IRS hauls just two or three high-profile citizens into court each year to make the terror show work on your mind.

Notice, they always pick citizens who follow silly theories, who make big bucks, and who attempt to get juries to see the semantic traps that Congress built into the law. Most juries won't follow the maze, and they'll be envious of the wealthy star or starlet who demands a multi-million-dollar tax refund. All the rest of us 67 million Americans who don't file also don't do kooky theories; we just obey the law as written. Oh – and *we don't ask thugs in a dark alley for refunds.*

I looked at all the things shown as taxable in the Code, and I found plenty of them. I started demanding that my employees at IRS show where I was made liable. They never can, yet their operations manual – and the law – demand that they do so. As long as they refuse to listen to me, their employer, I'm free to disregard the Tax Code as I disregard any other law that doesn't apply to me. Nowhere in the Code does it speak to my activities in specific terms, and that's exactly what the law demands. As you'll see below, the IRS employees' manual says what they're required to do.

I don't give a frog's quivering thigh what Dan Evans says; if my employees refuse to obey law, the burden of proof is not on me, it's on the crook. Bernie Madoff's line for all those years was *"trust me; everybody knows this is how it is."* Yeah, right, scum. Get your hand out of my pocket!

Racketeering has gone on in Congress for much too long; its IRS check-skimming scam must stop. In tens of million households including mine, it already has.

The law has *always* been on your side

In our system of self-government, We the People are the 'authorities' over government; it's every American's duty to know the basics of laws that affect us and of our Constitution, because we alone are authorized to enforce it, putting crooked government actors in prison.

As you read through the rulings below, notice that the federal courts have been on our side all along. I could have been free years earlier, had I known to read federal tax law and case rulings. Instead, I was terrorized by the tax industry and even by pastors, by CPAs who were very nice guys, and by others whose revenues are tied to tax write-offs.

Chapter 7

So Who *Does* Owe Income Taxes?

The individual, unlike the corporation, cannot be taxed for the mere privilege of existing. . . . The individual's rights to live and own property are natural rights for the enjoyment of which an excise cannot be imposed. Redfield v. Fisher, 292 P. 813, 135 Or. 180, 294 P.461, 73 A.L.R. 721 (1931)

To show a duty for an income tax, the government must first show a statute taxing some activity in which the targeted citizen is engaged; some privilege whose use the citizen enjoys.

The income tax is, therefore, not a tax on income as such, It is an excise tax with respect to certain activities and privileges which is measured by reference to the income they produce. The income is not the subject of the tax: it is the basis for determining the amount of tax. F. Morse Hubbard, as posted on Pg 2580 of the House Congressional Record (3/27/43)

In fact, the federal courts agree that common knowledge – the old 'everybody knows' doctrine – can't create legal duty; only operation of law or contract can do so: *The taxpayer must be liable for the tax. Tax liability is a condition precedent to the demand. Merely demanding payment, even repeatedly, does not cause liability.* Boathe v. Terry, 713 F.2d 1405, at 1414 (1983)

No matter how angry and terroristic they got, IRS couldn't create liability for me. I finally realized that these people are my administrative-branch employees, not some judicial body ruling over me. I knew that the IRS can't write laws; like you and me and every member of Congress, they must *obey* laws. So let's keep going down the rabbit hole, to see who the Tax Code says *does* have to keep records, file returns, and pay a tax.

Section 6012. Persons required to make returns of income.

(1)(A) Every individual having for the taxable year a gross income of the exemption amount or more...

39

Boy howdy...there was that word again. We saw what *individual* means as federal regulations define it...only in terms of *aliens* and since it *is* defined there and *nowhere else,* that is the binding legal definition of 'individual', for purposes of income taxes.

So the usual scare tactics – sections of the Code used by tax industry terrorists to 'prove' that I had to file and pay – those tactics always led back to legal bunny trails; traps that Congress built over two generations. I wanted to know, surely *some* people have to pay income taxes. Who *are* those people?

Since *taxpayer* is defined in 7701(a)14 as one who is *"subject to any internal revenue law",* the easiest thing is to just find a section or sections of the Tax Code making some people *subject* to it. The Supreme Court ruled that according to the Constitution, everybody *can't* be subject to it.

I repeat for the third time: According to the Tax Code, certain activities and domicile categories *do* have a liability to keep records, file forms, and pay a tax. That's a critical point you'll have to repeat as often as you discuss Tax Honesty with those seeking to keep the scam alive.

Some people *are* indeed made subject to the Tax Code, but *not everyone* is made subject. This means the Tax Code is constitutional, contrary to what some 'tax protestor' theories claim.

I found things that make a person into a 'taxpayer' as defined in the Internal Revenue Code; things that apparently create taxable income. In my decade of digging around in the Tax Code, I found a number of such activities and domicile situations; are your gainful activities here?

- If I live in D.C., Guam, Puerto Rico, or the Northern Mariana Islands;

- If I'm involved in manufacture or sale of alcohol, tobacco, or firearms;

- If I'm an officer or employee of the federal government;

- If I operate a merchant vessel;

- If I'm a nonresident alien or a principal of a foreign corporation with income derived from sources within the United States;

- If I'm a resident alien lawfully admitted to a State of the Union, the District of Columbia, or an insular possession of the United States;

- If I entered a voluntary withholding agreement for government personnel withholding either as an 'employee' (3401(c)) or an 'employer' (3401(d)) (See 26 CFR §31.3402(p)-1);

- If I've ever been notified by the Treasury Financial Management Service that I was responsible for administration of government personnel withholding (26 U.S.C. § 3403), or have applied for and received a Form 8655 Reporting Agent Authorization certificate;

- If I am an officer or employee of the Treasury or any bureau of the Dept of the Treasury subject to IRS authority related to submission of collected taxes delegated by Treasury Order 150-15;

- If I receive items of taxable income from foreign sources;

- If I receive foreign mineral income;

- If I receive income from foreign oil and gas extraction;

- If I receive income from a China Trade Act corporation;

- If I receive income from a foreign controlled corporation as fiduciary agent of the corporation;

- If I receive income from insurance of U.S. risks under 26 U.S.C. 953(b)(5);

- If I receive taxable items of income from operating an agreement vessel under section 607 of the Merchant Marine Act of 1936 as amended;

- If I receive items of income from a public works contract subject to Federal income and Social Security tax withholding;

- If I own stock in, do business with, or have anything else to do with a corporation in which the [Federal] United States of America owns stock. (See notes following 18 U.S.C. § 1001. Chapter 194, 40 Stat. 1015);

- If I receive wages or other compensation as an officer or employee of an oceangoing vessel construed as an American employer;

- If I receive gambling winnings from the District of Columbia or insular possessions of the United States;

- If I receive items of income from maritime (international) trade in alcohol, tobacco or firearms;

- If I receive items of income from production and/or distribution of alcohol, tobacco or firearms in the District of Columbia or insular possessions of the United States;

- If I receive any items of income from activities taking place within an 'internal revenue district' as such districts have been established under authority of 26 USC 7621 (U.S. Customs ports);

- If I receive items of income from maritime international trade in opium, cocaine or other controlled substances.

Boy howdy – so *many* taxable activities! But I never found *my* work in there anywhere. In fact, I haven't found in the Tax Code the gainful activities of the average American living and working in the 50 States.

I repeatedly demanded from IRS any citation of law that makes *me* a Taxpayer as defined in the Code, since so many other activities *are* mentioned specifically in it. But year after year, I only got *evasion* from IRS employees.

So when they made demands, I told them to pound sand. After the first few years, my terror victim conditioning wore off. After a decade of their evasions, they left me alone. I saw through their scam, and I've been a happy Nontaxpayer ever since.

Chapter 8

The Well-Settled Law

"The sky is blue" is not a *position;* it's a *fact.* All that you've read above, and that you'll read below, is not a 'position' or a 'tax protestor' theory. It is a long list of citations of *law* and rulings by America's highest court.

Just as I don't bother with federal laws about bulk pesticide disposal, nuclear power plant operation, or airline pilot training standards, I also don't care about the huge Tax Code because it doesn't apply to me or to most Americans.

But I will reiterate for the fourth time the heart of Tax Honesty; always remember it when you hear any 'tax protestor' theory, or any threat by a tax industry shill:

> The Tax Code *does* make some people subject to an income tax; *does* make some people 'taxpayers' as defined in the Code; I just reviewed a long list. But I am *not* on the list so I'm a happy, law-abiding Nontaxpayer.

Black's Law Dictionary Agrees

Black's Law Dictionary defines the legal principle *inclusio unius est exclusio alterius* as dictating:

Where law expressly describes a particular situation to which it shall apply, an irrefutable inference must be drawn that what is omitted or excluded was intended to be omitted or excluded.

Now, you just saw *many* sections of the Tax Code describing 'particular situations to which it shall apply', and since I could find nothing showing that *my* activities are likewise taxable, "an irrefutable inference must be drawn" that my income is *not* taxable.

The U.S. Supreme Court Agrees

Keeping in mind the well-settled rule that the citizen is exempt from taxation unless the same is imposed by clear and unequivocal language, and that where the construction of a tax law is doubtful, the doubt is to be resolved in favor of those upon whom the tax is sought to be laid. Spreckels Sugar Refining Co. v. McClain, 192 U.S. 297 (1904)

In the interpretation of statutes levying taxes it is the established rule not to extend their provisions, by implication, beyond the clear import of the language used, or to enlarge their operations so as to embrace matters not specifically pointed out. In case of doubt they are construed most strongly against the government, and in favor of the citizen. Gould v. Gould, 245 U.S. 151 (1917)

In view of other settled rules of statutory construction, which teach that a law is presumed, in the absence of clear expression to the contrary, to operate prospectively; that, if doubt exists as to the construction of a taxing statute, the doubt should be resolved in favor of the taxpayer... Hassett v. Welch., 303 US 303, 82 L Ed 858. (1938)

All of this well-settled law demands that in determining tax liability, nothing can be presumed taxable until finding in law what is *specifically indicated* to be taxable.

Sutherland's Rules Agrees

Recognized as a core text on statutory construction by the American Bar Association, *Sutherland's Rules of Statutory Construction* is a 10-volume exhaustive resource providing all the acknowledged principles of American statutory interpretation. In 66:1, entitled *Strict Construction of Statutes Creating Tax Liability,* I found the following, which is again precisely in line with a century of Supreme Court rulings just noted:

It is a settled rule that tax laws are to be strictly construed against the state and in favor of the taxpayer. Where there is reasonable doubt of the meaning of a revenue statute, the doubt is resolved in favor of those taxed. Revenue laws are considered neither remedial statutes, nor laws founded upon any public policy, and are therefore not liberally construed.

Even the Internal Revenue Manual Agrees!

Then I realized that even an unsigned, computer-generated demand for money can be *extortion*. When I've demanded to see the law I'm supposedly violating or a law that supposedly made me owe a tax, the IRS operative *must obey his/her operations manual* and show me the law:

4.10.7.1 Overview

Examiners are responsible for determining the correct tax liability as prescribed by the Internal Revenue Code. It is imperative that examiners can identify the applicable law, correctly interpret its meaning in light of congressional intent, and, in a fair and impartial manner, correctly apply the law based on the facts and circumstances of the case.

4.10.7.2 Researching Tax Law

Conclusions reached by examiners must reflect correct application of the law, regulations, court cases, revenue rulings, etc. Examiners must correctly determine the meaning of statutory provisions and not adopt strained interpretation.

4.10.7.2.1.1 Authority of the Internal Revenue Code

The Internal Revenue Code is generally binding on all courts of law. The courts give great importance to the literal language of the Code.

4.10.7.2.9.8 Importance of Court Decisions

The Internal Revenue Service must follow Supreme Court decisions. For examiners, Supreme Court decisions have the same weight as the Code.

So. If a section of law actually existed, how long would that take to dig up? *A minute or two?* Instead, no matter how often I asked the IRS, over a decade they repeatedly violated their operations manual and the law by engaging in extortion, and by demonstrating a pattern of *willful evasion.*

Chapter 9

Dealing With Administrative Branch Thugs

For 12 years, the first two of which I was still filing and paying their extortion, I noticed that IRS operatives invariably did one of two things when I demanded a response to that most basic question of income taxation. Either they passed the hot potato from one regional office to another like bullies in a playground, or they responded, 'we haven't finished our research; we'll get back to you' – *but then they never did.*

Every evasive non-response I received to my certified mail demands was additional evidence that they were engaged in *willful* evasion of law and of their own operations manual. If you watched any of the 2014 congressional hearings where IRS operative Lois Lerner lied through her teeth, repeatedly perjuring herself, you see how the IRS operates. See Appendix A for an article by the only official Historian of the IRS, exposing its utter criminality. But when you think about it, what do we expect from a state-sponsored terror organization: *lawfulness?*

I was Congress' willing dupe for 20 years. My 'tax evasion' was nothing more than obeying the laws while trying to escape Congress' financial fraud. I was trying to avoid financially supporting what I knew were massive violations of the Constitution. I was seeking to be free of the state-sponsored terrorism that allowed the D.C. Leviathan to grow like a cancer from the 17 enumerated, severely limited powers that we originally granted to our federal servants.

I *always* sent all correspondence to IRS by certified mail. I *always* kept hard copies and offsite electronic backups of everything. I'm not paranoid; just a former terror victim, educated and all grown up.

I was always factual, and my responses to their mail-fraud and terror threats were always cordial, but as firm as any employer should be when addressing a corrupt employee. No need for cursing or childishness; but no need to be a wimp, either. *They work for me,* not the other way around.

> The critical tactical point is this: if we're ever going to reverse the cancerous growth of the corrupt Deep State, every citizen should be willing to pay any amount due by law. If that amount is zero then I had to be willing to pay zero because by starving corruption we help to limit government to the enumerated duties that We The People assign it, in the U.S. Constitution.

Criminals at IRS masquerade as enforcement officers

I doubt that chasing thugs is a wise use of time, but if I wanted to go after extortionists at IRS just for grins, I'd begin by using this section of the Tax Code, since their manual says they MUST show the law under which they're trying to shake me down for cash. If they can't show the law, they're committing extortion:

Section 7214(a)

Offenses by officers and employees of the United States

Any officer or employee of the United States acting in connection with any revenue law of the United States (1) who is guilty of any extortion or willful oppression under color of law; or (2) who knowingly demands other or greater sums than are authorized by law ... upon conviction thereof shall be fined not more than $10,000 or imprisoned not more than 5 years, or both.

Please understand what that means: if you don't actually owe a tax by law and if you *never did* owe such a tax and never had a legal duty to file anything or keep records for government – then the public employee who keeps harassing you to 'comply' is just like any other criminal involved in fraud and extortion.

Taxpayers need to *read*...need to *learn truth* rather than be terrorized into thinking that a victim of terror is actually a 'criminal'. The situation is precisely the opposite; the 'tax cheat' is the woebegone citizen just trying to make sense of how America became communist China right before our eyes, in just one generation!

You are Hereby SUMMONED *(to the refrigerator box in my yard)*

Once I learned not to fear scary letterhead not backed by law, the fraudsters started looking pretty silly. For instance, I learned that an IRS 'summons' is just a piece of paper, of no legal consequence, as the federal courts ruled in 2005:

(A)bsent an effort to seek enforcement through a federal court, IRS summonses apply no force to taxpayers, and no consequence whatever can befall a taxpayer who refuses, ignores, or otherwise does not comply with an IRS summons until that summons is backed by a federal court order…[a taxpayer] cannot be held in contempt, arrested, detained, or otherwise punished for refusing to comply with the original IRS summons, no matter the taxpayer's reasons, or lack of reasons for so complying. U.S. 2nd Appellate Court- Schulz v. IRS (2005)

I could gain a 4-count indictment on IRS Thugs

Here in Texas we have it best of all. Texas law stipulates that it's a criminal offense every time the IRS sends a supposed 'summons' or anything else that can be construed by the citizen as originating from the judicial branch; that's the first criminal count for an indictment:

Texas Penal Code CHAPTER 32. FRAUD

32.48. Simulating legal process.

(a) *A person commits an offense if the person recklessly causes to be delivered to another any document that simulates a summons, complaint, judgment, or other court process with the intent to: (1) induce payment of a claim from another person; or (2) cause another to: (A) submit to the putative authority of the document; or (B) take any action or refrain from taking any action in response to the document, in compliance with the document, or on the basis of the document. (e) Except as provided by Subsection (f), an offense under this section is a Class A misdemeanor. (f) If it is shown on the trial of an offense under this section that the defendant has previously been convicted of a violation of this section, the offense is a state jail felony.*

The laws of Texas provide for a second count on the criminal indictment of IRS employees when they filed a 'Notice of Federal Tax Lien' in our Texas county records. As I learned, it was no legal lien at all; just teams of administrative employees, committing fraud by their manager's orders:

Texas Government Code 51.901.

Fraudulent document or instrument.

(c) For purposes of this section, a document or instrument is presumed to be fraudulent if: ...(2) the document or instrument purports to create a lien or assert a claim against real or personal property or an interest in real or personal property and: ... (B) is not created by implied or express consent or agreement of the obligor, debtor, or the owner of the real or personal property... (C) is not an equitable, constructive, or other lien imposed by a court with jurisdiction created or established under the constitution or laws of this state or of the United States.

Although it was not harming me, the IRS employees refused to get that NFTL fraud out of my county records back in 2004, so Texas law gave me a third count for a criminal indictment against the agency:

Texas Penal Code CHAPTER 32. FRAUD.

32.49. Refusal to execute release of fraudulent lien or claim.

(a) A person commits an offense if, with intent to defraud or harm another, the person:(1) owns, holds, or is the beneficiary of a purported lien or claim asserted against real or personal property or an interest in real or personal property that is fraudulent, as described by Section 51.901(c), Government Code; and (2) not later than the 21st day after the date of receipt of actual or written notice sent by either certified or registered mail, return receipt requested, to the person's last known address, or by telephonic document transfer to the recipient's current telecopier number, requesting the execution of a release of the fraudulent lien or claim, refuses to execute the release on the request of: (A) the obligor or debtor; (B) any person who owns any interest in the real or personal property described in the document or instrument that is the basis for the lien or claim. (b) A person who fails to execute a release of the purported lien or claim within the period prescribed by Subsection (a)(2) is presumed to have had the intent to harm or defraud another. (c) An offense under this section is a Class A misdemeanor.

Thus under Texas law, IRS commits a crime every time it files a 'Notice of Federal Tax Lien' against a Texan. If a court did not issue a judgment, then no lien can exist. Period. A notice is *not* a lien. No one is above the law in America!

Good luck going after federal mafia in a state court; I'm just showing you the law, not suggesting you try on your own, to go get federal actors indicted in your state courts. Bankers and mortgage companies in Texas should know the law. Instead, they violate their fiduciary duty to customers, and usually help the IRS terrorize them.

Of course it's only out of fear and ignorance, because everyone knows how honest the banking and mortgage industries are. And like the guards at the Nuremberg trials, Lois Lerner and all other IRS employees are only following orders. But now you've seen the provisions from the Tax Code and the Internal Revenue Manual. Ignorance of the law is no excuse for serial fraud and extortion, as defined in the IRM itself.

The fourth fraud count on the criminal indictment I could have asked the Grand Jury for is the IRS 'team signature' fraud. After looking at over a dozen copies of a Notice of Federal Tax Lien (NFTL) gathered from different people, I discovered one more IRS fraud tactic: every NFTL is signed in ink by one person using only first initial, and a second person's full printed name appears below the signature.

Is their up-line manager covering their tails in case they're caught? Both operatives can deny having actually filed the fraudulent 'lien' by just blaming the other signer. After thinking about going after the two IRS employees (both women, likely mothers) for criminal indictment, I got cold feet. I couldn't put someone's mom in federal prison since they didn't really harm me; only my reputation. But at least I had the goods on them and they knew it. If they ever brought me to court, I could have shown this Tax Honesty Primer to the jury.

I'm willing to bet that at least one out of any dozen Americans has the guts and brains to stand up to corruption. Not all judges are corrupt, either. The U.S. Supreme Court had this to say about government employees defrauding citizens:

This is the approach that has been taken by each of the Courts of Appeals that has addressed the issue: schemes to defraud include those designed to deprive individuals, the people...of intangible rights such as the right to have public officials perform their duties honestly. McNally v. United States 483 U.S. (1987) at 358

If I hadn't started reading a little law and doing a little digging, I would have been defrauded all my working life and a jury couldn't have helped me if I hadn't made copies of everything and seen what the IRS makes its employees do. I knew that before they could take any of my stuff, the crooks had to file that bogus 'lien notice'. I filed a public complaint right away when IRS tried to steal from me that way.

I filed an *Affidavit of Material Facts* (see Appendix B) with our county clerk. Every point in a signed, notarized affidavit that is not specifically answered is established in the record. I was then on the record that I only signed as 'Taxpayer' under penalty of perjury all those years out of ignorance and coercion.

After that, I informed my clients and the attorneys for my banks that filing an NFTL is *a criminal act* in our State. I sent my banks a certified letter informing them that if a fraudster claims funds in my account without a judge's ruling, I'd demand my full deposits from the bank or the FDIC just as if any other criminal stole my funds on deposit.

Chapter 10

Summary

To play offense as well as defense, consider joining AmericaAgain! and forming your <u>TACTICAL CIVICS</u> county chapter.

My prayer is that someday, We The People can bring Madisonian law enforcement to criminals who have turned Congress into their puppet theater, destroying American families, our national currency, and our once respected place in the world.

Congress' IRS Scam: Only the Tip of the Iceberg

Besides the Internal Revenue Code and the resources listed in the book above, I also recommend the books in Appendix C, to discover how deep the corruption is and how long it has been going on.

The pumping heart of American corruption is CONGRESS, not its tax collection agency. The IRS is merely Congress' mopping-up scheme to avoid hyperinflating the trillions in counterfeit 'money' it conjures up for itself every few months through its co-conspirator, the FED cartel.

You never learned history in school or college. The generation of Marx, Darwin, and Lincoln was America's watershed into tyranny. What most Americans think began in 1913, was brewing in the dens, offices, and clubs of powerful men for 80 years before Wilson's corrupt administration and the gangsters from Jekyll Island.

Congress passes 'laws' that industries write for themselves, then papers over the crimes with 'regulations' written by the industry itself, to supposedly control that industry. In the prosecutorial world, this is known as *capture*. Both political parties are corrupt organizations and the financial industry is almost entirely criminal.

The only way to re-capture Congress and federal regulatory agencies from predators is for We The People – through state criminal courts – to bust members of Congress for their criminal activities. They must choose between pleasing their billionaire handlers, and avoiding seizure of their assets and spending the rest of their life in a state penitentiary.

The IRS scam plays into this because 75% of federal activity is illegal according to the Constitution. The simplest first step to ending this massive bureaucratic cancer is to cut off its funding. How could we believe politicians' lies about 'smaller government'? As long as Congress skims every payroll account through its IRS scam, it will continue to haul in five times the revenues needed for its lawful powers!

If Americans want Congress to do more than the 17 things allowed it in the Constitution, the special interest must get an amendment to the U.S. Constitution ratified, following the process stipulated in Article V.

Corruption infests every government on earth; we can't eliminate it; but we can certainly *reduce* it. Rule of law prevailed as long as America had a Christian core of solid citizens willing to go after bad guys. But for over a century We The People have slept; perverts and greedy criminals have captured Congress and the federal courts, and have written the regulations that are supposed to liberate us from their predation.

The IRS debacle is run by the crime kingpins in Congress, who have been inviting and enabling this corruption. Now, a vital remnant of Americans will turn the tables on D.C. organized crime. AmericaAgain! and TACTICAL CIVICS™ will begin by restoring constitutional Militias in every county, training and briefing Grand Jury members on their amazing powers over corruption, and by seeking to get the original First Amendment fully ratified.

It was passed by Congress in 1789 and ratified by 12 states already. Only 11 were properly recorded, so it was technically ratified already in 1790, but needs to be ratified again, now by 27 more states; then it will become the 28th Amendment.

The amendment will require that congressional districts be a maximum of 50,000 people; that means small, low-budget elections so that citizen-statesmen can run for the U.S. House; you won't have to be a millionaire in the pocket of billionaires, to run for Congress. Best of all: the 31,000 American communities of under 10,000 residents will finally have representation in the U.S. House and the U.S. Electoral College for the first time in a century.

Anyone can join AmericaAgain! and launch a TACTICAL CIVICS™ chapter to turn the tide of history just when most Americans think our republic is finished!

Let Not Your Heart Be Troubled

In the almost 30 years that I've been a law-abiding Nontaxpayer, I've never been harmed by IRS or had one dollar taken by Congress' terror agents. I'm not suggesting that *no one* has; among us tens of millions of non-filers, many of them have war stories about skirmishes with the IRS. But many times more *filers* have such war stories. No American should ever fear his public servants! Your servants can successfully use terror to make you pay its demands only as long as you're ignorant and subservient to organized crime. Now, you need not be.

The 'Fair Tax' Trojan Horse

The law and the IRS can be left exactly as they are, with just one simple change: IRS employees must obey the law and not commit fraud or extortion. As Taxpayers grow more disillusioned with the corruption and outright theft by government at every level, they are easy prey for the politicians' pitch about a coming 'solution' that they call a 'Fair Tax'. Don't believe in the Tax Fairy; read powerful refutations of the scam in THIS article and THIS one.

Don't buy the Tax Fairy's magic dust. America would leap from the frying pan into the fire, after the lure of "getting rid of the IRS"; nonsense. Every retailer in America would be working for the IRS under that Trojan Horse scheme! Every proposal by a politician has a different plan for the same target: *your checkbook.*

The fraudsters in Congress have had the 'FairTax' scam waiting in the wings for many years. It's potentially an even *worse* scam than the one we're finally busting.

The Best Era in Our History

I pray that this booklet has been enlightening to you. What you do about Congress' tax scam is entirely up to you; this booklet is the record of my own experience, digging into the causes and strategies of earth's most powerful organized crime operation: the U.S. Congress.

We did not get into this corrupt mess overnight. I explain when, how, and by whom the mega-crimes were launched, in my other books including *This Bloodless Liberty, Fear The People, Tactical Civics, Mission to America, A Republic to Save, Grand Jury Awake, Tactical Civics™ High School Edition,* and hundreds of Training Center podcasts and blog articles.

Having to dig out of my self-imposed gulag of ignorance and fear led me and my brother to plant AmericaAgain! Trust, which has over 250 TACTICAL CIVICS™ county chapters so far (Nov. 2021) with the goal of having a chapter in each of America's 3,141 counties and county equivalents. Believe it or not, the open D.C. crime orgy of Russiagate, Shampeachment, the ChinaBatFlu gaslighting and forced-jab operation, and Election Steal 2020 only proves that we're entering the *best* period in our history: 150-year-old Marxism is finally dying a kicking, screaming death. It will not go without a fight; *but it will go.*

I know you agree with me, especially if you've traveled abroad: America is the greatest place on earth. I thank God every day that I live here, and you should, too.

But we have work to do, and I hope you'll join us in doing it.

Appendix A

The Most Secretive Institution
in federal government

by Shelley Davis Bishop

Reprint of an article by Ms. Bishop (nee Davis), the only official historian of the IRS in the institution's history.

For nearly eight years, I worked for the IRS. I did not process tax returns. In fact, I rarely saw tax returns. My job was unique for the tax collector. I was one of nearly 10,000 employees at the headquarters of the IRS in Washington D.C. , but I was the only one with the job title of historian. I turned out to be not only the first, but also the last, official IRS historian!

In the 1990s, my revelations of massive document destruction at the IRS, essentially the wholesale loss of the history of one of our most important government agencies, rocked the tax collector—at least for a moment. My revelations helped lead to congressional hearings and even a new law. Unfortunately, little has changed in the attitude or actions of the tax collector toward its record-keeping responsibilities for the American people.

Today, the IRS remains our most secretive and powerful federal agency. Without records, they remain unaccountable to Congress, but most of all to the taxpayers they pledge to serve.

After 16 years of working for the federal government as a professional historian, my career came to a jolting halt at the end of 1995 when I found myself facing allegations that I had wrongfully leaked sensitive information to a history professor from Franklin and Marshall College in Pennsylvania. While untrue—even laughable in retrospect—the lobbing of false charges against a federal historian aroused little concern among my fellow professional communities—historians, archivists, and records managers.

The story behind the false charges provides a fascinating and disturbing glimpse inside the workings of the IRS investigations staff. The trouble began with a FOIA (Freedom of Information Act) request filed by Professor John Andrew, who was searching for records related to IRS targeting of left-wing political groups during the Nixon administration. In his research, Andrew used transcripts of congressional hearings during the Watergate era and noticed specific IRS documents identified in footnotes. When his FOIA request asked for those records, the eagle-eyed investigators inside the IRS jumped to the conclusion that the only way that Andrew could know to cite specific documents by date, subject, and name of the author was if I had leaked such information to him.

Of course, the reality, sadly, was that the documents that Andrew sought, were destroyed by the IRS long ago. When two IRS special investigators drove to Lancaster , Pennsylvania to grill Andrew about how this information had been leaked to him by (obviously!) the historian, he simply pulled out his copy of the congressional hearing and pointed to the footnotes. As he explained this bizarre visit to me, he said, "I don't think those investigators had a clue what a footnote was!"

I live with my own personal sense of contentment that I did the right thing by resigning in protest when I learned of the false charges. I also live with deep disappointment that I was essentially abandoned by my peers simply because I worked for an agency that is considered to be of little historical importance or interest.

The years I spent with the IRS tell the story of a breakdown of federal records management when pitted against the powerful bureaucracy and intransigence of the IRS. The result of the untimely end of my federal historical career? The smattering or records from the IRS held by the National Archives increased slightly after my departure, primarily the result of the accessioning of three rooms of documents I personally squirreled away during my tenure. But there it stops.

My career sacrifice, I have decided, meant nothing in terms of reforming IRS records management, alerting the historical community to serious record keeping issues inside the government, nor increasingly the availability of IRS records to potential researchers.

Of course, this implies that someone out there cares about IRS records. How does one explain the nearly nonexistent reaction from the press, the public, and (most alarming to me) my professional colleagues in the historical community to my revelation that the IRS had systematically and intentionally (as well as unintentionally) destroyed its paper trail for the entire twentieth century?

Over the past few years, I have been forced to reach the disturbing, if self-evident, revelation. No one really cares. My sad realization is that as long as the tax collector doesn't reach into your own pocket, you don't give a hoot whether the National Archives has any IRS records. I was shocked to hear historians (yes historians!) nervously laugh, then tell me that perhaps it was a good thing that there were no IRS records because perhaps this decreased their chance of being audited.

Never has a federal agency—and its power—been so misunderstood by those we expect to monitor that power—journalists, historians, and record keepers. In the end, I concluded that the IRS—not the CIA, not the FBI, not the NSA—is the most secret of all our federal agencies. How can that be? Simple. Destruction of records is a far more permanent method of hiding from public view than stamping "Top Secret" on them and locking them away. There are no IRS documents from the 1930s or 1940s or 1950s waiting to be declassified. They're simply gone.

How could the IRS get away with shredding nearly their entire paper trail? Easy. No one was looking. The journalists were more focused on whether their mailboxes contained a notice from the IRS than on the tremendous investigative powers Congress has placed in the hands of this agency. Historians have overlooked the larger picture of the important role the tax collector has played in the forward march of American history, passing by the IRS as an uninteresting bureaucracy.

Somehow historians have failed to make the connection between tax collection and America 's financial, social, governmental, and military history.

But not only was no one looking over the shoulder of the IRS, another important element in explaining how we lost so much essential history is that the IRS outsmarted us all. While journalists and historians may have been oblivious to the power wielded by the IRS behind the scenes, the IRS was well aware of its own powers and the need to obscure them from public scrutiny. They took advantage of our naivete. They also held the ace in the deck—something called Section 6103 of the Internal Revenue Code. This is the section of the tax code that governs the confidentiality of tax returns; the clause that keeps your tax return between you and the tax collector.

Rather than using Section 6103 for what it was meant, i.e., protecting tax returns, the IRS took the convenient position that Section 6103 trumped everything else when it came to federal laws, rules, and regulations, including the Federal Records Act. This meant that the IRS swept its entire documentary trail under the realm of "tax return information," allegedly protected by Section 6103, whether or not a particular document had anything to do with tax data. Unwilling to take on the behemoth IRS (as well as lacking any push for access from any interested community), the National Archives and Records Administration turned a blind eye to this practice.

It has been a long and lonely ride for me to try to preserve and protect the history of our tax agency. The ultimate irony, I think, is that we celebrate our history as a republic which fought a war for independence based largely on issues related to taxation, yet we have let the history of the agency we created to enforce our own system of taxation, languish into virtual nonexistence.

The result, although we remain blissfully unaware of its potential consequences, is that we have granted the IRS powers above and beyond those of any other federal agency. One just has to wonder what the founding fathers would think of that!

Appendix B
Affidavit of Material Facts

This affidavit of material facts sets forth fact statements concerning my status and relationship to internal revenue laws of the United States and acts and omissions by Internal Revenue Service personnel that have adversely affected and are adversely affecting my substantive and procedural rights of due process as well as my inalienable rights.

The controversy involves alleged federal income tax liabilities for calendar year(s) (YEAR) through (YEAR). This affidavit is sworn and subscribed before a duly commissioned state notary public and therefore qualifies as testimony in all jurisdictions under the full faith and credit clause of the Constitution of the United States.

Fact statements are as follows:

1. My name is (NAME); I am a living, moral being endowed with unalienable rights to life, liberty and property, and all substantive rights secured by the Constitution of the United States and the Constitution of the State of (STATE).

2. I am a Citizen of (STATE), which is a State of the Union.

3. My abode and dwelling is geographically located in (STATE), which is a State of the Union.

4. I do not have a foreign tax home as defined in the Internal Revenue Code and am not subject to the Commissioner of Internal Revenue's authority delegated by Treasury Order 150-17 relating to foreign exchange of tax information.

5. I have never received notice from a District Director of an Internal Revenue Service district, nor the Assistant Commissioner of Internal Revenue (International), that I am or ever have been required to keep

books and records and file returns for any of the eight classes of tax administered by the Internal Revenue Service. (Letter 978 (DO) & Notice 555; see also 26 U.S.C. §6001, 26 CFR §§1.6001-1(d) and 31.6001-6 and Treasury Delegation Order No. 24)

6. I have not signed a Form 870 or any other examination agreement form. (See 26 CFR § 601.105(b)(4).)

7. Despite my request and/or demand, Internal Revenue Service personnel have not conclusively resolved contested matters of fact and law with a national office technical advice memorandum (26 CFR § 601.105(b)(5)) or any other comprehensive statement that includes findings of fact and conclusions of law. (See 5 U.S.C. §§ 556(d) & (e).)

8. I have never signed an agreement accepting examination officer findings. (See 26 CFR § 601.105(c)(1)(i))

9. I have never received notice that disputed matters of fact and law can be addressed via a national office technical advice memorandum in the examination for appeal format (See 26 CFR §§ 601.105 & 601.106.)

10. IRS examination and/or appeals officers have never provided me with findings of fact and conclusions of law that comply with requirements of 5 U.S.C. §§556(d) & (e).

11. IRS personnel have never affirmatively established IRS standing and venue jurisdiction in (STATE) on the record with documentary or testimonial evidence.

12. In the calendar year or years specified above, to the best of my knowledge, all of my income, regardless of nature or the activity from which it was derived, was from sources in (STATE) and/or other States of the Union.

13. In the calendar year or years specified above, to the best of my knowledge, all of my earnings and other forms of income were from private enterprise in (STATE) and/or other States of the Union.

14. I am not now and never have been a citizen or resident of the geographical United States, including the District of Columbia, Puerto Rico, the Virgin Islands, Guam, American Samoa, and the Northern Mariana Islands. (See definitions of "United States", "State", and "citizen" at 26 CFR § 31.3121(e)-1; see also definitions of "United States" & "State" at 26 U.S.C. subsections 7701(a)(9) & (10).)

15. I am not now and never have been a citizen or resident of the political coalition, compact or alliance of territories and insular possessions of the United States known as the [Federal] United States of America (not to be confused with the Union of States party to the Constitution known as the United States of America, established in the Articles of Confederation). (See notes following 18 U.S.C. §1001; 40 Stat. 1015, c. 194.)

16. I am not a nonresident alien, nor a principal of a foreign corporation, with income derived from sources within the United States. (See chapter 1 of the Internal Revenue Code generally; gross income "source" relating to items of income from taxable sources listed at 26 U.S.C. § 61 & 26 CFR § 1.861-8 generally.)

17. In the calendar year or years specified above I was not a person required to deduct and withhold a tax pursuant to 26 USC §1441.

18. In the calendar year or years specified above I was not a person "made liable for such tax" as specified at 26 USC §1461.

19. I am not a resident alien lawfully admitted to a State of the Union, the District of Columbia, or an insular possession of the United States.

20. In the calendar year or years specified above, I did not serve as an officer or employee of Government of the United States, the District of Columbia, or an insular possession of the United States, nor as an officer of a corporation in which the United States or the [Federal] United States of America has a proprietary interest. (See 26 U.S.C. §§3401(c) & (d) and 31 U.S.C. §9101.)

21. In the calendar year or years specified above, I did not receive

'wages' as defined at 26 U.S.C. § 3401(a) (See also, the Public Salary Tax Act of 1939.)

22. In the calendar year or years specified above, I did not knowingly and intentionally enter a voluntary withholding agreement for government personnel withholding either as an 'employee' (26 U.S.C. § 3401(c)) or an 'employer' (26 U.S.C. § 3401(d)). (See 26 CFR § 31.3402(p)-1.)

23. I am not a person subject to Internal Revenue Service tax audit and/or check authorized by Treasury Order 150-29.

24. In the calendar years specified above, I did not receive notice from the Secretary of Health and Human Services that I received or paid wages, as required by 42 U.S.C. 405(3), (4)(A), (4)(B).

25. I am not subject to and do not participate in the Northern Mariana Islands Social Security Tax administered by the Internal Revenue Service under authority of Treasury Order 159-18.

26. I have never been notified by the Treasury Financial Management Service that I was responsible for administration of government personnel withholding (26 U.S.C. § 3403), nor have I received the Form 8655 Reporting Agent Authorization certificate. (See Internal Revenue Manual §3.0.258.4 (11/21/97), January 1999 edition on CD.)

27. I am not an officer or employee of the Treasury or any bureau of the Department of the Treasury subject to Internal Revenue Service authority related to submission of collected taxes delegated by Treasury Order 150-15.

28. In the calendar year or years specified above, to the best of my knowledge, I did not receive items of taxable income from foreign sources (26 CFR § 1.861-8(f)(1)(vi)(A)).

29. In the calendar year or years specified above, to the best of my knowledge, I did not receive foreign mineral income (26 CFR §1.861-8(f)(1)(vi)(B)).

30. In the calendar year or years specified above, to the best of my knowledge, I did not receive income from foreign oil and gas extraction (26 CFR §1.861-8(f)(1)(vi)(D)).

31. In the calendar year or years specified above, to the best of my knowledge, I did not receive income from a domestic corporation that has an election in effect under 26 U.S.C. § 936 (Puerto Rico & possession tax credit). (26 CFR §1.861-8(f)(1)(vi)(E)

32. In the calendar year or years specified above, to the best of my knowledge, I did not receive income from an insular possession of the United States. (See 26 CFR §§ 1.861-8(f)(1)(iv)(F)-(H); see also, definitions of "State", "United States" & "citizen" at 26 CFR § 31.3121(e)-1 and "American employer" at § 31.3121(h)-1)

33. In the calendar year or years specified above, to the best of my knowledge, I did not receive income from a China Trade Act corporation. (See 26 CFR § 1.861-8(f)(1)(vi)(I))

34. In the calendar year or years specified above, to the best of my knowledge, I did not receive income from a foreign controlled corporation as fiduciary agent of the corporation. (See 26 CFR § 1.861-8(f)(1)(iv)(J))

35. In the calendar year or years specified above, to the best of my knowledge, I did not receive items of income from insurance of U.S. risks under 26 U.S.C. § 953(b)(5). (See 26 CFR § 1.861-8(f)(1)(iv)(K))

36. In the calendar year or years specified above, to the best of my knowledge, I did not receive taxable items of income from operation of an agreement vessel under section 607 of the Merchant Marine Act of 1936, as amended. (See 26 CFR § 1.861-8(f)(1)(iv)(M))

37. In the calendar year or years specified above, to the best of my knowledge, I did not receive items of income from a public works contract subject to Federal income and Social Security tax withholding. (40 U.S.C. § 270a)

38. In the calendar year or years specified above, to the best of my knowledge I did not knowingly own stock in, do business with, or have anything else to do with a corporation in which the [Federal] United States of America owns stock. (See notes following 18 U.S.C. § 1001; see also, Chapter 194, 40 Stat. 1015)

39. In the calendar year or years specified above, to the best of my knowledge, I did not receive wages, remuneration, or other compensation as an officer or employee of an oceangoing vessel construed as an American employer. (See 26 CFR § 31.3121(f)-6)

40. In the calendar year or years specified above, to the best of my knowledge, I did not receive gambling winnings from the District of Columbia or insular possessions of the United States. (See I.R.C. Subtitle D generally)

41. In the calendar year or years specified above, to the best of my knowledge, I did not receive items of income from maritime (international) trade in alcohol, tobacco or firearms. (See 27 CFR §72)
42. In the calendar year or years specified above, to the best of my knowledge, I did not receive items of income from production and/or distribution of alcohol, tobacco or firearms in the District of Columbia or insular possessions of the United States. (I.R.C. Subtitle E; 27 CFR §70)

43. In the calendar year or years specified above, to the best of my knowledge, I did not receive any items of income from activities taking place within an "internal revenue district" as such districts have been established under authority of 26 USC 7621.

44. In the calendar year or years specified above, to the best of my knowledge, I did not receive items of income from maritime (international) trade in opium, cocaine or other controlled substances. (See I.R.C. §§7302, 7325 & 7327 and 26 CFR §403)

45. To the best of my knowledge, I have never been involved in activity involving controlled substances subject to Internal Revenue Service investigation under authority of Treasury Directive 15-42. (See

26 CFR §403)In the calendar year or years specified above, to the best of my knowledge, I did not receive items of income from production and/or distribution of opium, cocaine or other controlled substances in the District of Columbia or insular possessions of the United States.

46. In the calendar year or years specified above, I did not knowingly and intentionally contribute or contract to contribute money, property, or other assets to the Treasury of the United States.

47. In the calendar year or years specified above, to the best of my knowledge I did not engage in any activity regulated under authority of Title 27 of the United States Code.

I attest and affirm that I have personal knowledge of all the facts stated in this Affidavit, and that they are true and correct and that they are provided under penalties of perjury under the laws of the State of (STATE), so help me God.

Further, Affiant sayeth not.

_____Signature

Date _____

Notary Certification

State of _____County of _____

On this date before me personally appeared (NAME), who proved to me on the basis of satisfactory evidence to be the person whose name is subscribed to the above instrument and acknowledged to me that (s)he executed the same in (his/her) authorized capacity and that by (his/her) signature on the instrument, executed the instrument.

Witness my hand and official seal, this _____day of _____, 2020.

_____Printed name of notary

_____Signature of notary

(Notary Seal)

Appendix C
A Reading List

My book *A Republic to Save: Essays in Tactical Civics* is a free 300-page PDF book, available free here. Don't let the size scare you; it's 46 brief essays. Skim the table of contents and just dip in to read one essay at a time.

Watch the 11-minute introduction to TACTICAL CIVICS™ HERE.

American history is fascinating; if we learn its lessons, we are not condemned to repeat them. To discover Congress' 150 year old criminal alliances with banking and industry, read:

Blood Money: Civil War and the Federal Reserve John R. Graham (2006)

Organized Crime: The Unvarnished Truth About Government Thomas DiLorenzo (2012)

The Case Against the Fed Murray Rothbard (1994)

The Best Way to Rob a Bank is to Own One William Black (2005)

It Takes a Pillage Nomi Prins (2010)

The Great American Stickup Robert Scheer (2010)

Griftopia Matt Taibbi (2011)

To learn exactly what the framers of the U.S. Constitution were thinking when they drafted and refined our supreme Law of the Land, read *Free, Sovereign, and Independent States: The Intended Meaning of the American Constitution* by John Remington Graham (2009)

The GOP has been a front for mercantilist criminals, born under Karl Marx's banner. Don't believe me? Read *Lincoln's Marxists* by Walter D. Kennedy and Al Benson, Jr. (2011)

.

Made in the USA
Coppell, TX
06 December 2021

67295855R00049